# a short & happy guide to

# Elder Law

By

## Kenney F. Hegland
*James E. Rogers Professor of Law, Emeritus*
*University of Arizona*

## Robert B. Fleming
*Attorney, Fleming & Curti, PLC*
*Tucson, Arizona*

## *Series Editor*
## Paula A. Franzese
*Peter W. Rodino Professor of Law*
*Seton Hall University School of Law*

## WEST.

Mat #41315017

Short and Happy Guide Series is a trademark registered in the U.S. Patent and Trademark Office.

© 2013 LEG, Inc. d/b/a West Academic Publishing

610 Opperman Drive
St. Paul, MN 55123
1-800-313-9378

Printed in the United States of America

ISBN: 978-0-314-28381-8

# Dedication

*Time held me green and dying*
*Though I sang in my chains like the sea*
Fern Hill, Dylan Thomas

*To Barbara and Rhonda*
*And to those who choose to sing*

# Table of Contents

## PART 5. DISABILITY AND DEMENTIA

## PART 6. FINANCES, MEDICAL CARE, AND HOUSING

## PART 7. ESTATE PLANNING

## PART 8. DYING - THE DETAILS

# A Short & Happy Guide to Elder Law

# Why a *Short* and *Happy* Guide to Elder Law?

*"Wow! I'm a lawyer; I even teach law; I'm a smart, educated guy. How can I be so stupid? Here I am, merrily going about my business, and hard times, they are coming, coming my way."*

This was my reaction when, well into my fifties, I started teaching Elder Law. I was shocked how little I knew of the problems I will face and my family will face. I became a nuisance, boring my friends and colleagues with the virtues of Living Trusts, with the necessity of Health Care Powers of Attorney, and with the compassion and love of Hospice.

I sat down with Robert Fleming, a lawyer who has spent his career representing seniors.

*"What are the problems seniors and their families are likely to face and how can they use the law to solve them?"*

We wrote a book. It was too long, too detailed, and too boring. Folks who needed the information weren't getting it; families would suffer without having a resource to turn to. We decided to do this book—shorter, less detailed and, hopefully, spiffy.

Our audience: law students and lawyers, counselors, health care workers, folks who work or volunteer at Area Councils on Aging or Adult Care Centers, indeed anyone who helps seniors. Seniors and their families will also find the practical guidance handy and we occasionally address them directly.

Whoever you are, skim the book, pause to read what catches your eye, note what you may need to come back to. You will be better informed and more apt to tackle the challenges that lie ahead; guaranteed.

We offer a lot of practical advice. Law takes you only so far.

*Happy?* We want you to be better prepared for things that go dump in the night and a book on the shelf does no good at all. Fred Rodell, a law professor at Yale, once wrote:

*There are two things wrong with almost all legal writing. One is style. Readers like a dash of pepper or a dash of salt along with their information. They won't get any seasoning if lawyers can help it. Lawyers would rather be dignified and ignored.*

We won't be ignored. We will lighten your load with bad jokes and good poetry. Our topics do not immediately lend themselves to "happy." Late night comedians do not open with riffs on "How to talk to your family about end-of-life matters." Yet us humans are blessed to see a glimmer of humor even in the darkest of times:

*Art Buchwald, newspaper man, was dying of kidney failure. At one point he decided to go off dialysis knowing that he soon would die. He gave one last interview to his old friend, Tom Brokaw.*

*"Art, what will you miss most?"*

*A pause, some thought, and then "Global warming."*

# PART 1

# Some Basics

*C H A P T E R 1*

# Working with Seniors

Avoid first names and (worse yet) condescension. "Mr. Peterson" and "Mrs. (perhaps not 'Ms.') Blaine," not "Charlie" or "Rose," and never "Dear" or "Honey." Strive to be warm and friendly, but professional.

You will need to be clear. Your client may have difficulty hearing you, or reading your brilliant writing. Talk slowly and distinctly, but do it without being obvious. Do not shout. Do not ask clients if they have trouble hearing—they will claim that they do not, but may be insulted by the suggestion of infirmity.

Don't cover your mouth while talking, or turn away your client. Pay attention to physical arrangements: are your chairs too firm or too soft, or too low, or too hard to get up from? Is your conference table arranged so your clients see you in a halo of light from the bright windows? Are you talking past your client to their adult child, or caretaker, beside them?

Connect personally. A casual question might work wonders. "Do you remember when President Kennedy was shot?"

Delivering twins on a commune in Maine, coaching football in Lubbock, getting a PhD in Berkeley. What a great opportunity you have to hear incredible, interesting stories. There is more wisdom and humanity in those stories than in all the best-sellers.

Most of all, like they used to say, *respect your elders.* Though they may actually be happier than you (studies confirm this), they are facing problems you may have heard about but likely never experienced. Later we'll try to give you at least some idea of what it is like to grow old. Realize however that *knowing* is not *experiencing.* Aging is not for sissies. There are more-or-less constant aches and pains, death of long-time friends, and the background noise of chariots hurrying near.

*"What would you like to accomplish?" "Do you see any problems with that?" "Any alternatives?"* Get their thinking before offering your own. Get it from them—don't assume that their children, or even their spouses, know exactly what they want you to do for them. Don't stereotype folks, thinking they all want the same things and are facing the same problems.

Make sure your advice is understood and remembered. You are an expert in your field and it is hard to recall what it was like when you were first learning the ropes, when you nodded to the teacher, "Yes, I understand" when you hadn't a clue. What seems clear to you, what seems painfully obvious, just ain't. Explain. Ask the person to repeat your advice, thus assuring it was understood and will be remembered. It may also flag things you didn't cover: "Does that mean I have to change the beneficiaries on my IRA, too?"

Follow up letters are great. Use a large and readable font, (studies indicate that sans serif fonts are easier to read, and that sizes between 12 and 14 tend to be optimum), consider double spacing, use short sentences and paragraphs, and use the active voice. Avoid bold, italics and all-caps, or use them sparingly.

*Folks in the room* can help understand, and recall, your advice. However, there are problems. As a technical matter it breaks the attorney/client privilege. More basically, it might impede candid conversation, and too often family members simply cannot resist the desire to answer your questions rather than wait for the senior's answer. You are representing the *senior,* not the family member or friend that brought the person in. Explain that you are ethically obligated to meet with your clients alone and ask the others to wait outside. Hear your client's authentic voice before allowing family members—even those with impeccable intentions— to participate. This is particularly true if you are discussing the senior's estate plan.

*Decisions.* They're theirs, even the stupid ones. However just don't sit there. You're a counselor not a scribe. Current choices may result in future trouble: the estate plan that treats the kids unequally without clear reasons, the decision to put grandma in the first available nursing home, the "I'd rather not talk about these bruises."

*How intrusive?* Your client has asked about whether she needs a Will but you know she might face other issues—she might be caring for a family member with a disability, or raising a grandchild.

*"Tell me something about your family situation."*

*"How are things?"*

This may trigger,

*"I'm a little worried about my mother. She might have Alzheimer's."* Or *"My son has never gotten a good diagnosis, but he*

*just doesn't seem to be able to make it in the world. He can't understand money, can't even make change."*

In the next chapter we suggest a *legal checkup*. Like a medical checkup it is designed to make sure that there aren't other pressing issues.

*Competence.* One must be able to see and evaluate options. Some talk of one's *executive function*: the ability to speculate about the future and make rational plans. "If you wanted to go the Hawaii, how would you go about it?" If the answer is "Ask my son," there may be trouble. Generally, folks who are concerned about losing mental competence are less of a worry than those who think all is fine. One of the hallmarks of diminishing capacity is the inability to see limitations as they develop.

*Getting used to it.* At first you may be uncomfortable around older folks. They're old and maybe disabled. At some point they will die. Think of all you will learn from them, learning about life by listening to those facing death. Morrie, of *tuesdays*, said:

*"To know you're going to die, you can be more involved in your life. Once you learn how to die, you learn how to live.'*

# CHAPTER 2

# A Legal Checkup

*"Now that we've discussed the specific concern that brought you here, I have some general questions that might disclose some problems I can help you with or, if not, make a referral. Shouldn't take more than a few minutes. Kind of like a medical checkup. Is that O.K.?"*

This checklist is also an introduction to the book. The questions will trigger your curiosity.

*Are you on the internet?*

This might be the most important question of all. Being on the internet opens new worlds, entertainment, education, health information, finding old friends. Local libraries and senior centers offer courses. Of course newcomers must be warned of internet frauds. Along these lines, "Any problems reading?" Tablets with back lighting and font enhancement can bring back the joys of reading.

*Questions concerning needed Documents*

Someone in your family, due to a physical or mental disability, might not be able to make good decisions. Do you have documents that will help?

*Medical decisions*: Living Will, Health Care Power of Attorney

*Financial decisions*: Joint accounts, Living Trusts

*Questions concerning estate planning*

Any changes in your family, divorces, remarriages, births of children or grandchildren, that may impact on your Will, Trusts, or IRAs? Have you reviewed you Will or Trust in last five years? Is there someone, like a grandchild or mentally disabled relative, you would like to give money to but hesitate fearing they would waste it?

*Questions concerning a family conversation?*

Have you talked with your family about the elephant in the room, possible disability, funerals, and end-of-life decisions? These difficult conversations are the best gift you can give your family.

*Questions concerning quality of life*

Some folks have a tough time in retirement, lying around the house all day, not getting exercise. Some begin to lose it either physically or mentally. It is a bad mistake to think this is an inevitable part of aging or that it is within the person's control. Often a lot can be done to improve their quality of life.

*Questions concerning home care*

Has your home been made as safe as possible?

If you are caring for someone, are you getting enough rest?

If you are being cared for by an adult child, do your other children know how expensive and difficult it is? Do they know your caregiver may be entitled to a tax break?

Have you considered moving to a retirement home?

*Questions concerning health*

Any problems with sleeping or hearing? Memory loss? Drug or alcohol use?

*Questions raising touchy points*

Is anyone in your family still *driving* when you think they shouldn't be?

Are there *guns* in the house? (Suicide is always possible.)

Do you fear that a relative may be abused? Can you visit, alone?

As to phone solicitations, have you gone to "Do-Not-Call"? Have you learned to hang up and that it can be OK to be impolite?

*Questions re grandchildren*

If you are raising your grandchildren do you have documents authoring you to deal with doctors and schools? Have you considered adoption so that the decision to return the child to the parents is yours, not theirs? Have you contacted Social Security concerning possible support?

*Questions concerning last illnesses*

If an aged relative is in the hospital have you and the doctors confronted the possibility of death? Whether surgery and continued treatment are the best options? Have you considered hospice, not just in the last week of life but in the last six months of life.

Have you learned to spit? (We'll tie this up.)

# CHAPTER 3

# What Folks Are Going Through

---

*Three tough things about growing old: First, you're not as spry. Second, you forget things.*

People are living longer, in better health. "Happiness" surveys put seniors as the most contented. But we have not come to praise old age. Physically, seniors lose strength, flexibility, balance and stamina; mentally, some memory and some ability to learn new things; socially, long time friends become infirm, move away and die.

Add to these slings and arrows, going to reunions only to discover that none of your classmates have come, only their grandparents.

Why do seniors cut so easily? Why do faces wrinkle? Fewer cells. Babies are so cute, so plump, so lovable, because they are bundles of cells. Cut them and they heal instantly. Over time, cells die. (This is good; if they refuse to die they become cancer.) This does not mean that seniors can't be buff. With exercise, the cells we have can be made larger, but those we have lost are not readily replaced.

Along with cell loss comes a general decline in physical prowess—heart and lung capacity shrink. Gray hair? Beginning around age 30 hair follicles produce hydrogen peroxide, blocking the follicles' ability to make melanin, the pigment that gives hair its color. (In a terribly misguided apology, Mother Nature tries to make up by sprouting vast amounts of hair on your ears.)

*Weight gain.* Metabolism slows. Looking at the generation before us, we might get it wrong "Those folks are skinny." But that generation was *always* skinny (unlike, alas, us). Cross-generation comparisons are dangerous: in Miami, for example, one would conclude that most folks are born Cuban, die Jewish.

*Hearing and vision.* Expect losses. There are things to be done, but vanity may get in the way. That same vanity creates problems for the attorney, too: if you ask "Can you hear me OK?" the answer will almost always be "yes" regardless of hearing limitations. Instead try asking: "Which side can you hear me better on, and I'll sit on that side."

*Sex.* Viagra attests that sex is well and thriving. In nursing homes this presents something of a problem (or not).

*Short-term memory loss.* "Senior moments"—are to be expected. "Why did I come into the front room?" "Where did I put my keys." Gaffes, falls, and lost keys are no longer shrugged off as they were before; they now seem to signal ominous things. But short-term memory lapses don't often lead to severe memory loss. Many remain mentally active and agile in advanced old age despite occasional lapses. While your client might laugh and make remarks about "senior moments," you shouldn't. In our household we have what we call the "my mother" rule: I can make fun of my mother's foibles, but it is off limits for the rest of the family. Same here. Clients may not enjoy your remarks about memory shortcomings as much as they enjoy making them.

*Personality changes.* Some get grumpy. Discomfort trumps charm; small talk might be hard if one is worried about one's next doctor's appointment. Economists have a less forgiving explanation: there is less need for charm as you age. As you no longer need to impress employers and friends, smiley faces are no longer worth the effort. Maybe people aren't *getting* grumpy; they were *always* grumpy but hid it.

Being old used to be special, valued. They looked dignified, told wonderful stories, taught younger generations how to make things work and, in times of trouble, provided wise counsel. What happened?

Dignified? Millions and millions of dollars went to convince us that gray hair and wrinkles are ugly, to be avoided at all costs. And, thanks to terrific advances in public health and medicine, older folks are no longer rare, they're everywhere, crowding the malls, taking their sweet time turning left, and bankrupting Social Security. As for their stories, they don't come close to MTV and HBO. As to their knowledge and wisdom, they published.

The senior citizen may no longer be a player. Waitresses say "dear," cheerful young men hold open the door, and family members will think all they are interested in are Social Security, current illnesses, and, on a good day, maybe your grandkids—never mind politics, books, movies and, yes, sex and romance. People treat you as a child—as someone who needs constant advice and constant help. Recall how that felt: "Mom, I can do it myself!"

However, there is some good news in all of this. The negatives don't come suddenly and totally, they sneak up. You get used to them. While we tend to think good things will be better than they turn out to be (think of being disappointed with highly praised movies), we tend to think bad things will be worse than they turn out to be. Is growing old insufferable? Nope. *Studies have repeatedly shown that older folks are generally happier than younger ones.*

Why not? Freed from the restraints of adulthood, no longer the teacher on the playground, again the kid. Free to sleep in, to wear trousers rolled, to eat a peach, and to disturb the universe (or perhaps, less grandly, the neighbors). British poet Jenny Joseph summed it up: when she's an old woman she will

*Make up for the sobriety of my youth.*

*I shall go out in my slippers in the rain*

*And pick flowers in other people's gardens*

*And learn to spit. . .*

# PART 2

# Advice for All Seasons

# Confronting the Elephant

*Oscar Wilde's reported last words: "My wallpaper and I are fighting a duel to the death, one or the other of us has to go."*

Few families talk about the elephant in the room, the possibility of disability and the certainty of death. These talks need not be grim and are vastly more important to family happiness than a bushel, indeed a barrel, of legal documents.

Starting the talk is hard. We recommend first writing a letter to the family, to collect thoughts and topics, have the family read the letter and go from there. Here is one possibility with commentary.

*Dear Folks,*

*If there comes a time I am quite sick and unable to make my own decisions, I want my family to make them for me.*

While everyone should have a Living Will usually doctors defer to the family's wishes. This makes sense. Often Living Wills are filled out years before they come into play and, when they do, one's family, *if it knows the person's general wishes*, will have a better feel for the actual situation—how old the patient, how likely the recovery, how painful and expensive the treatment, and how the person's favorite team is doing.

> *If my family can't agree it's up to Kris who has my Health Care Power of Attorney.*

We'll have more to say about Health Care Powers of Attorney downstream. Here we simply note that is probably the most important document to have.

> *I realize your decision might be to "pull the plug" and remove me from all life support. Nurses and doctors have assured me that dying from a lack of hydration is not a bad way to go. At some point that is absolutely the right decision. Keeping me alive beyond that is not an act of love. Don't keep me alive simply because no one wants to face the bad news. Insist that my doctors tell you my chances of recovery, how long it would take, and what would be my condition afterwards. A good question to ask, "Would it surprise you if he died in the next month?"*

In Oscar Wilde's play *The Importance of Being Earnest,* it develops that Earnest had died after his doctor had given him only "a short time to live."

"He seems to have had great confidence in the opinion of his physician."

Doctors are reluctant to give bad news. Trained to save lives, it's very hard to give up. In *Final Exam* Dr. Pauline Chen writes:

> *Even medicine's essential framework for approaching clinical problems—the treatment algorithm—presumes physical ac-*

*tion. For every point along the algorithms there are several possible outcomes that in turn may have several of their own therapeutic options. On no branch of the decision tree, however, is there a box reserved for Do nothing or Hold tight or Sit on your hands.*

And when doctors do give bad news studies have confirmed the obvious: families often don't hear. The result: far too many die lingering, painful and expensive deaths.

*If I am in a bad way insist that I have a DNR (Do Not Resuscitate) Order as Code Blue works great on TV but not in real life. Be leery of surgeries which will cure a specific problem but will not extend my life, causing pain and leaving me groggy.*

Except on TV yelling "code blue" and "step back" seldom saves lives. Usually those orders cause pain and broken ribs. As for surgeries, a study of Medicare patients who died showed that nearly 1 in 3 had surgery in last year of life, nearly 1 in 5 in last month, nearly 1 in 10 in last week of life.

*I can live without walking but don't want to live if I can no longer appreciate my family and friends and can no longer understand the world around me.*

This is a good time to reflect on life. Dr. Groopman writes we focus on the negative consequences of disability, on what will be lost after colostomy, prostrate surgery, mastectomy. But this *"focusing illusion neglects our extraordinary capacity to enjoy life with less than 'perfect' health."* We think things will be worse than they turn out to be.

*I'm a wimp when it comes to pain. Tell my doctors to give me enough pain meds even if it means they might kill me; that's my choice and my family supports it.*

Health care workers may not give sufficient pain medication out of fear of causing addiction or fear of professional or governmental discipline. Fortunately there is a new speciality, *"Palliative Care"* which in no longer restricted to hospice patients.

> *If there comes a time that my driving endangers myself or others, I want my family to tell me. I'll be mad but I don't want to end my life by killing someone.*

> *If there comes a time that I must move in with one of you, I want the others to realize how difficult and expensive my care will be. They should also take turns giving the caregiver some time off.*

Caring for disabled relatives is extremely hard and quite expensive. Far too often family members not involved in the care complain that the care giver is wasting money.

> *Families fight over who gets the Grandfather Clock. Get together and write a list of who gets what.*

Elder law lawyers agree that most bitter family fights are not about money but about who gets family heirlooms. *Written lists* avoid "She said" "No she didn't."

> *My Will is with my lawyer, Victoria Blair. My other important papers are in the desk, the one next to the Grandfather clock.*

> *I want to die at home or in a hospice. Short stays in ICU are okay to stabilize my condition and figure out what to do. Donate what you can of me.*

We will have a lot to say about the wonderful hospice movement. Three quick things: it is not just for cancer patients, it can be done at home, and some people get better and walk away. Far too many never avail themselves of hospice or wait until the last weeks of life. Think of it, not as "giving up," but as "being comfortable and cared for."

As to burial, cremation and Irish Wake. But don't let cousin Joe speak.

Now that you have read this, sign off:

We family members have read this and we agree to follow it.

_____

Once the family reads and signs, time for the talk. Remember A.E. Housman:

Malt does more than Milton can,

To justify God's way to man.

# CHAPTER 5

# Confronting the Angst

Existential angst. *The feeling that nothing matters, that all is lost, that the best one can do is to sit before the TV, eating potato chips.*

Retirement can be rough, some live the existential angst we only read about in Philosophy 101 (before that night's party). The solution? Work, volunteer, study, pump iron.

We want to help others. Better than, "Do this, it will help *you*," is "Do this, it will help your *family*."

*Working*

*A store greeter is reprimanded, "George you're doing a wonderful job. People love you. But you are always late. When you were in the Navy, what did they say when you came in late?"*

*"Good morning, Admiral."*

Many businesses hire older folks, either full or part time. One downside. If the person has taken early Social Security and is still under his or her full retirement age, their the Social Security check will be reduced one dollar for every two dollars earned over $14,000.

## Volunteering

> I am of the opinion that my life belongs to the whole community and as long as I live, it is my privilege to do for it what I can. I want to be thoroughly used up when I die, for the harder I work, the more I will live. George Bernard Shaw.

Volunteering need not be full time. Often there are one-day opportunities. Try *Area Agencies on Aging* and www.national service.gov—type in an interest (veterans, education, elderly) and zip code and, like magic, scores of possibilities appear.

Volunteers should check to see if they are covered by the organization's *liability policy* and, if not, whether state law shields them from civil liability except for acts outside of their job and for willful or wanton misconduct. If part of the job requires driving one should check to see if their auto insurance will cover such activities.

Volunteering is more than its own reward. After six months volunteers at an elementary school did significantly better on mental tests than the non-volunteers (and they lost weight!). Learning new tasks, meeting new people, does the trick (or maybe it was simply sitting in small chairs).

## Learning

Learning new things, working crosswords, playing computer games, all have been touted as a way to ward off mental decline and dementia. While recent studies suggest that physical activity may play a greater role than mental activity, learning needs no cheer leaders; it is its own reward.

Community Colleges and Senior Centers offer courses on movies, history, crafts, computer skills, etc. The Bernard Osler Foundation supports senior learning in 170 colleges and universities. Book clubs are one possibility, particularly for men who generally retire with no friends.

Travel helps. Making plans, reading maps, finding good restaurants, learning Greek for "Where's the bathroom?

*Pumping Iron*

Physical exercise might be the best way to keep mentally sharp. As with all scientific explanations, it is easy to understand: exercise releases something somewhere which makes its way to the brain to interact with something else which then does something not yet clearly understood which stops the brain from shrinking. Researchers have concluded that by walking one can regain some lost brain matter, that of a 65 year-old now that of a 63 year-old (people years, not rat years).

Some weight work is good. Muscle loss leads to difficulties in getting out of chairs and increased incidence of falls. But *walking* is key. According to Blue Cross Blue Shield, a person walking 10,000 steps a day will lose weight, lower cholesterol, and reduce the risk of heart attack. Our own doctor refers to daily walks as "The Fountain of Youth." Of course Blue Cross is only thinking of you, never mind the billions it would save. Think of the fabulous impact on mental abilities, the concentration required to count those steps, "Eight thousand, five hundred, fifty-one; eight thousand, five hundred, fifty-two; eight thousand, five hundred, fifty-three; eight thousand, five hundred, fifty . . . fifty? Darn! One; two . . ." Want to improve your elderly clients' lives: buy a batch of cheap pedometers and hand them out.

Most can reach the magic figure of 10,000 steps by adding a *30-minute walk* to one's daily routine. That's a lot. Work up to it. Most people stop exercising because they were too ambitious when they started. "30 minutes? I'll do 40!" "Well, I did 40 yesterday so I can skip today." Best to start with five. "Wow, that was easy. I'll go a little further tomorrow."

If you can't work in a 30 minute walk, recent research suggest that *three ten-minute* walks, spread through the day, are just as effective. Dr. Oz recommends at least a 7 minute workout. (Everyone can spare 7 minutes and most everyone can last that long.)

With all of this hype about the virtues of exercise, however, one might hear: "Hey Grandma, why aren't you out running a marathon?" Her response: "Why aren't you out running a four-minute mile?" Some just can't and some simply don't want to. These folks are not "generation-slackers." Disability and illness may hamper some, and, as we age, our interests may change: just as we are no longer interested in becoming a movie star, we may no longer be interested in brisk walks, physical fitness, or sweat.

"Enough already!" One can have a good life even if you don't play tennis, do water aerobics, or smile continuously.

# CHAPTER 6

# Making Things Safer

Age sneaks up. Homes may no longer be safe.

*Folks fall.* Are rugs secure? Rugs need sticky rubber backing, and yet they should be thin enough to make it easy to navigate over them—even with a cane, walker or just heavy feet. Does the shower have slip-proof mats? Grab bars? Professionally installed are best; see a Surgical Supply company for referral. Light-weight tables flip when used to help get up. Toys (grandkids' or pets') on the floor? Chairs really need arms.

*Folks lose night vision.* Are there enough night lights to get from bed to bath?

*Folks lose strength.* Do the chairs have arms to help getting up? Grab bars near the toilet and bath? Toilet seat raised?

*Folks lose reaction times.* Is the hot water heater set so that it will not produce scalding water?

*Folks lose track of time.* Large clocks in each room help orient.

*Folks have emergencies.* Smoke and carbon monoxide detectors? Are phones accessible? Cordless phones may be better. Cellular phones? Maybe, but consider how easy it will be for an unfamiliar senior to navigate on-screen buttons when panicked, groggy or confused. There are commercial home alert systems available which allow calls for help, including the always-stylish panic button worn as a necklace or bracelet and set up to automatically summon help through a 24-hour call center.

*Folks have aging eyes.* A fascinating body of research suggests that many of the problems associated with aging, such as memory loss, slower reaction time, insomnia and even depression, are possibly caused by *aging eyes* which filter out blue light. Does the home have bright indoor lighting? Skylights? Extra fluorescent lights?

*Frayed and overloaded wiring causes fires.* Surge protectors help. (A local bar would not serve string — stay with us. A string tied himself in a knot and entered. "You can't come in here. You're a string?" "No, I'm frayed not." This gets boring for us too.)

*Structural changes* may be needed (wheelchair ramps, widened hallways, modified bathroom facilities). Landlord *must* allow these changes as long as it is agreed they will be removed later.

An occupational therapist can be quite helpful in making specific suggestions. For example, if the elder is a gardener but has knee or hip problems, raised plant beds can work wonders. Someone with bad arthritis will find level handles more friendly than door knobs.

*Pets.* Pets should stay even if they're trouble. They are most important to the quality of life and changes in the environment are confusing. If there are no pets, consider getting one, perhaps a therapy dog, one trained to be gentle, to simply hang out, and to be little trouble.

*Guns.* This is a very sensitive subject and if you ask if the there is a gun in the house best make clear that you are not a government agent, making a list. No doubt having a gun makes many feel much safer in their home. However you can urge gun owners to keep them in a safe place away from grandchildren. One disturbing statistic, given the frequency of depression among seniors: according to a 2002 Centers for Disease Control and Prevention analysis, guns are the method of choice for 73% of suicides among those over age 65.

# PART 3

# Daily Troubles: Getting In and Out

<br />

CHAPTER 7
# Grandchildren

---

*Remember "Goodnight Moon" and the little old lady whispering "Hush"?*

*Fat chance.*

### Raising grandchildren

Nearly six million U.S. children live in a grandparent's home, and another two million in the homes of family members other than parents. About ten percent of those have no parent living in the household with the grandparent or other family member. The phenomenon of "grandfamilies" has become widespread, and many seniors are taking care of grandchildren.

There are lots of resources for the grandparents. A few stand out: "Generations United" (www.gu.org) and the AARP's "Grandparent Information Center" (www.aarp.org). Both provide lots of information, tips and local references. Local programs are available; the biggest needs are often respite care and legal advice.

*Legal Problems.* Physical custody is not *legal* custody—doctors, dentists and principals may require *parental* consent. For

<br />

<br />

28

*temporary stays,* say over the summer or until the parents can relocate, the parents should notify doctors and school officials. Many states permit a short-term (usually six months or a year) designation of someone to act on behalf of a parent—the document might be called a "Power of Attorney" and statutory forms are often available. A backup "To It May Concern" letter should help as well (notarized is best: bells and whistles always impress the reluctant.)

In cases where parents are unavailable or unwilling to act, a *guardianship* may be necessary. This involves court filing and, in most states, some monitoring by the courts. A guardianship based on the parents' consent (or their failure to object) will probably automatically terminate if either parent writes to the court revoking consent, so there is a impermanence about these guardianships.

Guardianship often does not require any allegation of the parents' unsuitability; that may be initiated in a juvenile *dependency* proceeding. Once juvenile court has become involved it is (in most states) much harder for parents to terminate the custody arrangement. It is also likely to be a much more closely-supervised arrangement, with long-term court oversight.

If the custody change is going to be permanent *adoption* should be considered. Without it the grandparents and the child are subject to the whim of the parent suddenly reappearing years later to take the child. Some states have "permanent guardianships" but *adoption* is the best choice. One caveat: adoption is permanent, and if grandparents hope that their child will get better and be able to take the grandchild back, they should probably not pursue it.

If a grandparent is caring for a grandchild, good planning should include nominating a successor to take on the role. For that matter, if a senior is caring for any other family member (spouse, child OR grandchild) who is unable to make care decisions because of age or disability, the senior should include a transition plan as part of their estate planning. While not binding on the court, it is essential to nominate a guardian in one's will.

*Finances.* Social Security benefits may be available for grand-children—even if not adopted. Children of retirees, including adoptive children, under 18 (or disabled), may be entitled to benefits. So too grandchildren being raised by a grandparent who dies or becomes disabled. Local welfare offices and Area Council on Aging might have good tips on finding needed support. There is abundant information (in a searchable format) on the terms of Social Security benefits available on the www.ssa.gov website.

## Making gifts to grandchildren

Grandparents are often confused about the effect of making gifts to their grandchildren. There are a number of tax and practical considerations—and on top of that the ever-present concern that giving money away might be imprudent if it turns out you need it for your old age. Some of the rules about making gifts:

*Taxes*: there is no income tax deduction for making a gift, and no income tax is paid by the recipient. There is a potential gift tax consequence for making a gift over a threshold amount (currently $13,000 per donor, per recipient, per year—in other words, a husband and wife can give each of their grandchildren $26,000 each year with no tax consequence whatsoever). Above that threshold figure there probably will be no tax due, but a return should be filed.

*Uniform Transfers to Minors Act (UTMA)*: Usually the larger problem is not taxation but how to make the gift. A minor is by definition legally incapacitated—they often can't open a checking account or even cash a check (though banks and state laws may allow smaller amounts with parent or custodian involvement). One solution is to utilize the *UTMA*, some version of which has been adopted in nearly every state (two states still use the older, but similar, *Uniform Gifts to Minors Act*). Think of the UTMA statute as creating a simple statutory trust, with a trustee (called "custodian") and automatic termination date (usually age 18 or 21, depending on the state and the source of the money). One big issue with UTMA accounts: they have to be listed on the "Free Application for Federal Student Aid" (the much-dreaded FAFSA) when the child applies for college aid.

*Section 529*

Speaking of college aid, there is a relatively new player in the gifts-to-minors arena—the "Section 529" plan which provide a great opportunity for grandparents to make simple, cost-effective gifts with a focus on education—the very thing grandparents often want to see their grandchildren receive. Visit the recognized authority on the genre: www.savingforcollege.com.

*Inheritance*

To leave money to a grandchild one needs a Will or Living Trust; only in the rarest of circumstances will they take under a state's intestacy law. Besides, since a minor grandchild can't receive an inheritance directly, leaving money outright to the grandchild forces the family into court-supervised conservatorship (or guardianship, depending on state terminology). If grandchildren are intended beneficiaries, more careful planning is required.

*Visiting Grandchildren*

In some unhappy families grandparents are not allowed to see their grandchildren. Most states have laws that allow judges to order grandparent visitations over the objections of the parents.

These are very narrow as much discretion is given the parent. Counselors work better than lawyers here.

*Death of a parent*

When a parent dies, the survivor automatically assumes legal and physical custody of the child, even if there has been a prior divorce which gave custody to the other parent. If both parents die, the Probate Court will appoint a guardian for the child and usually, but not always, the court will follow the wishes of the parents expressed in their Wills.

*Abused or Neglected Grandchildren*

Report fears to Child Protective Services. They will investigate. The reports are confidential. If fears are confirmed, there will be a court hearing with the State as the moving party. The judge may order counseling in the hopes of keeping the family together or remove the children temporally to live with other relatives or foster parents while the parents work out their problems. In extreme cases parental rights may be severed and the children put for adoption.

# CHAPTER 8

# Divorce and Remarriage

*Divorce*

*I promised to be with you in health and sickness, in good times and bad, but not for 24 hours a day.*

Retirement triggers problems. Daily routines must be renegotiated and long suppressed emotional problems, often having nothing to do with the marriage, may suddenly poison relationships. For example, some Vietnam veterans are showing up in PTSD clinics; horrible memories, suppressed during their working years, come rushing back in retirement.

Divorce is usually a disaster. Counseling, or separate bedrooms, are the first choices. From a legal standpoint probably the only two times a divorce makes sense are when one wants to remarry or when one needs governmental assistance under programs such as Medicaid (BUT note that divorce is seldom a positive even in the long-term care Medicaid situation—read on).

Why a disaster? Lawyers might put it this way:

Representing murderers I represent bad people at their best, representing divorce clients I represent good people at their worst.

Most states have "no fault" divorces allowing them for "irreconcilable differences" (although lawyers still like to cast blame as a way of impacting the contested financial aspects). As to *property* distribution, state laws differ, with a few following the old Spanish tradition of *community property,* while most follow the English tradition of *dower.* While there are nice theoretical distinctions between the two, as a practical matter most judges (and state divorce laws) will try to *split* the property acquired during a long-term marriage. This is easier said than done.

Dividing the *family house*? Unless there are enough assets to allow one party to buy out the other, the house will have to be sold. Dividing a *pension plan*? If both parties are retired, that isn't too hard but if one is still working the future value of the plan must be projected and then reduced to *present value.* Economists love this, what with color charts and computer print-outs. They bill in *current* dollars. To solve these difficult problems, some states allow the judge to simply order that one party receive, at the time of the other's retirement, a percentage of that retirement. Federal law allows this to be done for Military benefits as well.

A quick note on Social Security. After a divorce, at the age of 62, the non-wage earner can collect on her ex-husband's Social Security account if (1) they were married at least ten years, and (2) she has not remarried. If she remarried after the age of 60, she does not lose eligibility.

If one of the parties is the bread winner, there will be the matter of *alimony,* now called *spousal maintenance.* The basic notion is to "maintain" the non-working (or less-earning) spouse at relatively the same standard of living. But good luck for either party to live at their previous standard.

Divorce seldom protects the well spouse against long-term care costs. Since the assets will have to be divided, the spouse living at home is likely to end up either owning the family home and not much else OR relatively cash-rich and homeless. Besides, the well spouse could conceivably even be required to pay spousal maintenance to the spouse with long-term health problems—and that could even prevent eligibility for Medicaid. In most cases the couple with one ill spouse will end up better-off financially by staying married and taking advantage of their state's modest ac-commodations to Medicaid needs for couples.

What about health insurance? If one spouse is covered by the other's policy, divorce will likely end that coverage, or dramatical-ly increase its cost.

Finally, divorce doesn't make one any younger.

How to avoid all of this? Separate bedrooms. No need to di-vide property, to obtain additional health insurance, or to pay lawyers.

Another alternative is a *legal separation.* It can provide for a formal settlement of economic issues while allowing for the con-tinuation of health and death benefits. Under a legal separation, the parties are still married.

Finally, something we have all wanted to know. Does sex con-tribute to marital problems? Probably not. Senior sex in the words of one expert can be "frisky, frequent and fun." In fact, frequent sex correlates with better health. Of course, this raises a chicken and egg problem, which came first, the sex or the health? A cartoon shows a chicken and an egg lying in bed, smoking, one is asking . . .

### Remarriage

*Second marriages represent the triumph of hope over experience.* — Samuel Johnson

If hope *never* triumphed over experience lawyers would be out of work. Here it triggers a batch of new tasks:

1. Rewrite Wills and Trusts.

2. Review IRA beneficiary designations, property and bank accounts held in joint ownership and notify Social Security.

3. Tote up assets and liabilities—with some emphasis on things like your first spouse's Irrevocable Trust and your ability to change ultimate distribution of assets.

4. Consider a prenuptial.

5. Tell the kids.

Rewriting legal documents every five years or so is a good idea in any event: *"You mean I was leaving money to that worthless bum?"* Rewriting them at time of remarriage is essential; otherwise fights are certain down the road.

There is a special problem with *blended families*, where there are *children from prior marriages*. Usually newlyweds rewrite their Wills, leaving their estate to the other and, at his or her death, the reminder of the estate going to the children of each. How can one be sure the new spouse (now grieving spouse) will keep the bargain and not write a new Will? Betrayal! Shakespearean tragedy!

*Tear my Will, a thousand pieces,*

*I leave it all to my portly nieces!*

This is not a knock on spouses but an acknowledgment of how conniving portly nieces can be. *"They never visit you and they stole a lot from the estate anyway."* A *Living Trust* is a good solution. All the property goes in the Trust for joint use; when one dies, the Trust becomes *irrevocable*, with the income going to support the survivor and then, at the death of the survivor, the remainder going to the kids.

A *"prenuptial"* is simply a written agreement between the happy couple (while they still are). It can cover such things as:

1.  Who is responsible for the debts brought into the marriage?

2.  In the event of divorce, what happens to the property brought into the marriage *and* to property acquired during it? What of support obligations?

3.  Who is to inherit what?

4.  Who takes out the garbage?

Number four is not a joke (at least not much of one). We all get set in our ways. Marriages require adjustments. It might be well to hammer some things out—such as vacations, hobbies, relationships with ex's, and things of that ilk. These concerns may seem petty, but they are the stuff of life.

To make a prenuptial legally enforceable, as there is the potential for overreaching and misunderstanding, *each party* should be represented by separate lawyers. *Full disclosure* of assets and debts must be made; otherwise, a court will throw it out.

Prenuptial agreements can be important. At death, and despite what the new Will might say, the new spouse may be entitled to half the property earned during the marriage and, in some cases, some of the property brought into it. If the marriage ends in divorce, a spouse will be entitled to division of the property and perhaps maintenance unless there is a prenup waiving these claims. Of course, if a lot of money is involved, expect a fight as to the validity of the prenuptial agreement. Unlike death and taxes, prenups ain't certain.

Now the tricky part: "Hey kids, I'm getting remarried." Good luck with that. Nothing changes. Over 150 years ago the English novelist Anthony Trollope nailed it:

> *The idea that their fathers and mothers should marry and enjoy themselves is always a thing horrible to be thought of in the minds of the rising generation.*

Not every new romantic or sexual relationship requires marriage. Plenty of seniors live together without marriage – often for years and sometimes for decades. There are often good financial and emotional reasons for such a decision. Learn to probe and do not take appearances for granted.

# CHAPTER 9

# Sex and Driving

But not at the same time.

*Sex*

*"George is hot stuff here in the nursing home. We ladies love him, fight over him. He can dance . . . and he has his teeth."*

Unfortunately this is not a product placement paid for by the dental floss industry. Nor is it a ploy to increase book sales by appealing to prurient interests (at least not totally). Sex continues.

In Arizona the retirement community of "Sun City" is known as "Sin City." On the web you can find "Senior Dating Services." A study of healthy people, aged from 80 to 102, found that 88% of men and 72% of women have sexual fantasies and 66% of men and 38% of women continue to have sexual intercourse. And sexually transmitted diseases, at least those not transmitted by toilet seats, are still hard to discuss with one's doctor.

Sex, as always, is more than sex. It is a statement of contin-ued involvement with life, a source of emotional support, and a validation of self-worth. It may not be your grandchildren's sex; it might be simply caresses and gentle touching. Self-help manuals abound describing elder-friendly techniques.

Competent consenting adults, in privacy, can do what they want. Recently the Supreme Court underscored that right by strik-ing down a Texas statute that criminalized gay sex, holding that it violated the Due Process Right of privacy. *Forced sex* is criminal. Consent obtained by threats, tricks, force, drugs or booze is not consent. Nor is the "consent" given by someone legally unable to consent, children under the age of 16 or 18, and mentally impaired adults.

*What about individuals with dementia?* A *non spouse* having sex with such a person could not claim 'consent" and could be criminally prosecuted. But what about the *spouse*? We doubt very much that one would be prosecuted; in such a case the court might recognize a defense of "prior consent."

Forced sex, in addition to being a crime, is a tort. This means that the perpetrator can be sued for money damages. Not only can the perpetrator be sued, but so too anyone who had a duty to pro-tect the victim but didn't.

All of this straightforward law pretty much means a headache for the administrators of George's nursing home. He and the ladies who fight over him have a right to do what they wish and a nursing home that attempts to prevent that is demeaning their person-hood. However, the picture changes if George is forcing himself on the ladies or if he is having sex with women who, due to dementia, do not have legal capacity. In these two cases, George is guilty of sexual assault and the nursing home, under a duty to protect its residents, may be sued.

How nursing homes handle the situation varies a great deal. All will attempt to prevent *non-consensual* sex and some will rat to family members if a resident is engaging in consensual sex. Some, realizing the therapeutic good flowing from relationships, openly discuss geriatric sex.

Just as sex hangs in there, so too love. Sandra Day O'Connor retired to help care for her husband who, suffering from dementia, was living in a continuing care facility. She discovered that he had fallen in love with another patient and, realizing his happiness, she willingly stepped aside.

She was a wonderful Supreme Court Justice as well.

### Driving

*I want to die like my grandfather, quietly in my sleep. Not like his passengers, screaming in the back seat.*

Drivers over 75 have more fatal accidents than any other age group save teenagers. Add a little dementia and elderly drivers are 7.5 times more likely to crash, exceeding the rate of even drunk drivers. Why? Slower reaction time, heart attacks, impaired vision, particularly night vision, dementia (getting confused about where one is, and forgetting one has agreed to stop driving).

### Staying alive

The AARP offers a refresher course ("55 Alive"). There is an online program, *DriveSmart*, which offers a series of exercises will make you (it is claimed) a better driver. It's costly, about $100. Commercial driving schools offer programs as well. While these courses certainly cannot hurt, and may help individual drivers, there is (sadly) little evidence that the functional driving abilities lost with normal aging can be compensated for by training, even specialized training.

Special equipment is available, such as rear mirrors that provide a wider view of the road, and cars and vans can be outfitted to cope with many disabilities. Certain medications can affect driving ability. Check with the doctor or pharmacist. Trip planning helps. *Avoid rush hour, left turns, and frequent trips.* Co-pilots help.

*Convincing someone to stop driving*

A lot's at stake. Driving was the mark of adulthood; getting behind the wheel, we became the master of our fate. Giving up signals a loss of independence, vitality, and control. Many live far from shopping, churches, movies, restaurants, and friends. Public transport is often infrequent. Without wheels life may become afternoon TV and a quick decline into depression and illness.

Much better than "You should stop driving today" is "You'll have to stop driving in four or five months. Will you agree to stop then?" If you can get the agreement best to write it out and have it signed.

Legal sticks help. "If you kill someone you're stuck. If a judgment against you exceeds your insurance coverage, the person you injured can come after your life savings. It is no defense that you'll go on welfare. And if you are driving my car, I might be liable as well, for negligently allowing you to do so."

Of course one should appreciate the position of the elder. Without driving, how can one get to shopping, movies, church? Come up with a transportation plan.

Family doctors might help and many states require a field driving test for elders. Private evaluators are available.

Simply suspending the license will not stop every driver. Plates can be removed, keys hidden, and spark plugs disconnected.

The good news is that there are a growing number of programs that provide seniors transport. There are programs where the family car is donated to the agency which in turn provides taxi services. There is a national movement fostering what is known as Supplemental Transportation Programs (STPs). They are run by local governments, churches and non-profits. The Area Agency should have information on them. A prime mover in the movement is the Beverly Foundation and information can be found at www.beverlyfoundation.org.

Retirees, still good drivers, can volunteer to drive.

No peeling out.

# CHAPTER 10

# Scams and Identity Theft

*You can fool some of the people some of the time—and that's enough to make a decent living.* — W.C. Fields

But for W.C. Fields' great line we would have skipped this chapter. We'll keep it short.

*Victims should scream.* It's not their fault; doesn't show they're losing it; doesn't mean they're incompetent. MBAs from Harvard get cheated, only for a lot more money.

Contact the *Consumer Affairs Office* in the state's Attorney General's Office or County Attorney's Office. *Law suits* are possible. State laws prohibiting consumer fraud may give victims not only the right to get their money back but also to sue for damages. Attorney fees may be recoverable. *Small Claims Court* is another possibility. Easy forms, no need of a lawyer, telling the judge what happened. Large corporations can be sued and usually they can't bring their lawyers.

*Identity theft*

Thieves get account numbers (Social Security, credit card, bank), open accounts, run up bills, and, unless they are very new to the game, don't pay them. They go through mailboxes, garbage, invade computers, work in offices that have numbers, and some even get numbers the old fashioned way: stealing wallets and purses.

*Never* trust *unsolicited* emails, letters, or phone calls. No bank, financial institution, or governmental agency, *will ever request that one send them financial information.* (Crooks will.)

*Don't keep Social Security cards in wallets or purses. Some routine forms (doctor offices, department stores) have blanks for Social Security numbers; leave them blank.

*Shred important documents. Buy a crisscross shredder. Keep important documents (tax records) in locked files. Identity thieves may be relatives, colleagues, visitors or, we kid you not, plumbers!

The Federal Trade Comission's identity theft hotline is

1-877-438-4338.

*Scams*

"Sorry, I can't talk right now, my house is on fire."

"Sorry, I can't talk right now, I'm giving a commencement speech."

These ploys never work. Phone solicitors have heard them all before.

"Have you saved the cats?" "Will you tell the graduates to hold on to their dreams or go to law school?"

Once they get you talking you're a goner. Many are simply too polite to simply hang up. They have to get over that. If they haven't already: Do Not Call List: www.donotcall.gov/; 1-888-382-1222, TTY 1-866-290-4236.

A new scam is *relative* or *friend in trouble.* A call from a granddaughter who needs $500 immediately or she will spend the night in some horrible jail. Or an email from a friend claiming to be in Europe without funds as he has been robbed. These contacts may seem legitimate—scammers can get a lot personal information from Facebook.

*Alert from Chase Bank Security. Third parties have attempt-ed to access your account. We will have to suspend your ac-cess to your accounts, unless you send us, immediately, your Social Security number, your account and PIN numbers, your date of birth, your mother's maiden name, and your favorite flavor of ice cream.*

This is known as *"phishing."* The bait comes in many forms: "alerts," "updates for your credit union," "unauthorized activity warnings," "immediate cancellation of your trading privileges." Their emails look quite official and some purport to be from the U.S. Government.

*Home Mortgage Scams.* Crooks offer loans (door-to-door, by mail, through the internet) allowing one to pay off bills and requir-ing only low monthly payments. Lower payments do not mean low-er interest; they mean a longer time paying back the loan.

*Health Care Scams.* Apricot pits don't cure cancer. Fraudulent cures cost money, delay cure, and kill. No matter the ailment, from cancer to wrinkles, from alcoholism to ulcers, someone offers a miracle cure. The American Medical Association advises *extreme caution* if the cure is claimed to be *quick and easy* or that it involves a *"secret"* formula or machine to cure disease.

*Home Repair Scams.* Folks claiming to be city inspectors show up to check for violations. Will Rogers, or his double, offers a *free* roof or furnace inspection. Dollars to donuts the home will need repairs.

*Lottery Scams.* A letter or email announces winning $2,000 in the Canadian lottery (which you never entered but hey!). To get your winnings simply send back $200 or bank information.

*A hotdog stands next to his mailbox, opening a letter. "Congratulations, you are a wiener."*

*For further tips, go to eldercare.gov and get "Protect Your Pocketbook." The FTC.gov has information on charity frauds.*

By the way, the chances to win Powerball are 1 in 146.1 million; so even if you buy 73 million tickets, it would be even money that you would *still* lose, and, if you *did* win, good luck finding the winning ticket!

# Discrimination in Housing and Employment

Boss: *Sorry about the disability, have to let you go.*

Boss: *Sorry, old goat, you're fired.*

Landlord: *Sorry, no goat.*

Seniors facing adverse job action on the job based on age or disability may have a claim under federal law. In the case of housing, age discrimination is legal under federal law but not disability discrimination. But discrimination against goats? It's known as a teaser.

A few quick points. While we focus on federal law, many states have parallel anti-discrimination laws which may provide for broader relief ("more money"). Most are enforced by governmental agencies. It is easy to report discrimination and let them investigate. But one has to act quickly or the Statute of Limitations will bar action.

## Age Discrimination in Employment

*Mandatory retirement* was outlawed when Congress passed the Age Discrimination in Employment Act (ADEA), the narrow exceptions dealing with matters of public safety; for example, airline pilots. It also protects people 40 and older from discrimination in terms of hiring, firing, promotion, and pay and applies to part-time and temporary workers as well. This law applies to almost all employers (private and public, profit and non-profit) but only if the employer has *20 or more employees*.

Employers can fire for bad job performances, even if those poor performances are due to the aging process. Employers can reduce the work force, as long as they do not single out the elderly. But they cannot simply assume that no elders can do a job simply because some elders cannot. Individual decisions must be made. It is a violation of law to have a *job requirement* that is not really needed if it acts to discriminate against the elderly.

Workers who are fired or quit before their retirement benefits vest forfeit those contributed by their employers (employees get their contributions back but the employers keep those they contributed). Workers who are fired or are forced to quit due to miserable working conditions (constructive discharge) may have a claim.

Seniors get sick more and to avoid higher insurance premiums a company might refuse to hire or might fire (or force into retirement, or make life hell so that they quit) older workers. This is against the law. Employers can, however, insist on spending the same amount on all employees. This may result in lesser coverage for older workers; the same premium will get more coverage for a younger worker than for an older one.

*Disability Discrimination in Employment*

The Americans with Disabilities Act (ADA) protects disabled individuals in employment. An employer must make "reasonable accommodations for *known* physical or mental limitations of an otherwise qualified individual," for example changing the height of desks, giving additional training, or more frequent rest breaks. They need not incur unreasonable expenses. Small employers are exempt from the ADA: those with fewer than 15 regular workers.

Disabled individuals may also face discrimination in government programs (no programs for the deaf in school) and public accommodations and facilities (no ramps in retail stores). Contact the federal Equal Employment Opportunities Commission (EEOC), which enforces the ADA, or the state's Attorney General's Office.

*Disability Discrimination in Housing*

Under the ADA it is illegal to refuse to *rent* or *sell* to a person because he or she is disabled, an individual who has a "physical or mental impairment that substantially limits" one of the major life activities, such as walking, unless the handicap is such as to threaten the health and safety of others or would lead to substantial property destruction. The only housing exempted from the ADA is single dwelling residences rented or sold without a Realtor; small housing complexes of four or fewer units where the owner occupies one; and housing run by religious organizations and private clubs.

It is also a violation of federal law to refuse to rent or sell to a tenant because of race, color, religion, sex or national origin. Those protections are provided by the Civil Rights Act of 1964.

*An Important Note to Disabled Renters.* They have right, at their expense, to make *reasonable modifications* (for example, put in ramps or grab bars, or lower or raise counters) to accommodate

the handicap if they agree to restore the place to its original condition.

Disabled victims of housing discrimination can contact the
federal Department of Housing and Urban Development (HUD), or
a state housing enforcement agency.

But wait! What about "Old Goat" discrimination?

*Old Goat Discrimination*

*Assistance animals* must be accommodated in nearly all housing (not just government-subsidized housing). Service animals are
not categorized as "pets," and in most cases a person with a recognized disability is entitled to keep an assistance animal in their
rental unit. No formal training is required to make your dog an
assistance animal, and emotional support is one of the services
such an animal can provide. The practical reality may be that the
assistance animal category is limited to dogs, cats, and the occasional trained simian.

As to pets, owners of *federally assisted housing*, designated
for the elderly or disabled, cannot have flat rules against pets. The
landlord can prohibit pets which are a nuisance or a threat to the
health or safety of others.

So no lions, crocodiles, or T Rex. Dogs, cats, goldfish fine. Old
goats? Discuss.

# CHAPTER 12

# Dealing with Doctors

*"Now, what I want you to do, right when you get home, and this is very important, is to qubt twri pzcv jmottm plbtk!*

Most fain understanding, not wanting to make trouble, not wanting to look stupid, not wanting to seem "losing it." Studies have confirmed that many patients leave without understanding the advice or, even worse, getting it wrong. (Studies have also confirmed that the sun sets in the West . . . usually, you never know about tomorrow.)

Our advice: *Repeat the advice!*

*Repeat the advice!*

This does three things. It assures that one got it right, it helps memory, it fills in gaps: "Should I take those two pills together?"

*Take Aunt Margaret*

Doctors do not like others in the room during the exam, but, when it comes to the discussion of diagnosis and treatment, it is

52

good to have someone there to recall the information and occasionally, to act as the patient's advocate.

*Being heard*

> *The defendant is complaining to the judge. "I want a new lawyer. This one never pays any attention to me."*
>
> *"What about that, Counselor?"*
>
> *"Sorry, Your Honor, I wasn't paying attention."*

Professionals aren't good listeners. They ask questions, we answer them. They are the experts, after all. Doctors interrupt their patients in the first *18 seconds* of the visit. (There was a study!)

Patients must get their stories out. One doctor advises his colleagues: "If you listen to your patient, he is telling you the diagnosis."

*Preparing*

Take a list of medications (including over-the-counter). A prioritized list of concerns helps; the real one, the embarrassing one, shouldn't be last. As to internet research there are some good sites which can sharpen questions and make the most of the doctor's advice.

But beware TV ads suggesting ills we didn't know we had and telling us of the medicine we very much need (after downplaying that it will likely lead to suicide). The drugs they push may not be right and, for sure, more expensive than those that are just as effective.

*Errors patients make*

Seniors often ignore *weight loss* and *sleep loss* thinking nothing can be done. These can be serious and can be treated.

Another common error is to generalize from specific instances. *"Uncle Tom had the same condition and he took Brand X and got better. Give me Brand X."*

But maybe Uncle Tom didn't have the same condition; maybe he would have gotten better without Brand X; maybe he came within an inch of suicide.

*Errors doctors make*

It's flu season. You wake up with the classic signs: fever, cough, aches and pains. What do you conclude? Flu. You're not alone. Probably your doctor would too. "A lot of that going around." Both of you might be *wrong*.

In a terrific book, *How Doctors Think*, Dr. Jerome Groopman warns that doctors often misdiagnose, perhaps 1 out of 10 times. Like the rest of us, they jump to conclusions. To make sure they haven't, Dr. Groopman recommends we ask three questions:

1.  *What else could it be?* ("Well now that you mention it, it could be . . .")

2.  *Is there anything in the exam or tests that doesn't fit?* ("Well, now that you mention it, your fever isn't typical.")

3.  *Is it possible I have more than one problem?* ("Well, now that you mention it, sometimes folks get the flu because they are already sick with . . .")

A good friend, Dr. Jack Boyer, suggests a fourth question:

4.  *Have you considered whether I want to get the treatment or not?*

*Tests*

Nothing worse than a long wait to get the results. Ask, "How long before I hear?" and "Should I call?" *Call.*

*Serious illness*

There will come a time where one must consider hospice and end-of-life. Don't expect your doctors to volunteer dismal information. In *A Death Foretold,* Dr. Christakis tells us that doctors shy away from terminal prognosis. It undercuts their sense of professional competence, their belief that they can cure most anything. Many are uncomfortable with the idea of death and fear making self-fulfilling prophecies. The result:

> *"The great majority of Americans die in institutions rather than at home as many would prefer; most die in pain while in the care of health providers; many die alone; and many have deaths that are financially devastating for their families."*

If the physician isn't talking about death doesn't mean all is rosy. Finally one more agonizing question.

> *Would it surprise you if this patient (my mother, me) died within the next few months?*

# CHAPTER 13

# Abuse, Neglect, and Financial Exploitation

Elders are abused in the best of families, in the worst of families; on Baltic and on Boardwalk. And it gets worse, not better, more frequent, more severe. It does not self-correct—intervention is imperative.

*Visit often and insist of details*

Most of the physical violence suffered by the elderly is inflicted by spouses, with husbands being the more frequent victims but wives the more severely injured. Often the abuse is of *recent* origin. Retirement requires couples to work out whole new ways of living. Conflicts happen and old scores settled. Some Vietnam vets, after suppressing PTSD symptoms during their working years, find them rushing back when they retire. Alcohol abuse becomes more common and care giving is extremely stressful.

*Abusers keep victims isolated.*

"Mildred's a little too tired to come to the phone just now."

"Mildred, isn't it a shame your son never calls?"

Don't dismiss *complaints* as grumpiness or discount bruises, burns, welts, cuts, punctures, sprains, broken bones, dehydration, weight loss; missing eyeglasses, hearing aids, or dentures. Abusers will explain these away as the results of falls or illnesses. Insist on details by asking them to explain exactly how and when things happened.

Insomnia, excessive sleep, and change in appetite may indicate depression and hopelessness due to *psychological abuse*. So too can tearfulness, paranoia, low self-esteem, excessive fears, ambivalence, confusion, resignation, or agitation.

Other signs of abuse come, not from the victim, but from the *caregiver*. Is the caregiver drinking? Depressed? Resentful? Overworked? Or, alas, driving a new car?

*Get the victim talking*

Many fear retaliation or abandonment by the abuser. Some victims blame themselves, thinking they deserve it, and some believe that being abused shows that they can no longer run their lives, that they are getting senile.

* *"I'm concerned that someone may be mistreating you. I know this is very hard for you to talk about. Let me tell you a few things that might address some of your fears. Abuse is found in all kinds of families and it's not your fault. I won't think less of you no matter what you tell me."*

* *"You may fear what's going to happen to you if your caregiver gets into trouble. There are ways to protect you and get you someone else to care for you."*

* *"Abuse gets worse, not better. Even if the person has prom-ised never to do it again."*

As to *financial* abuse, look for the sudden inability to pay bills, withdrawals of large amounts of cash, and living well below one's means. Children steal ("Well, I'll get the money later, any-way."); home-care workers steal. It is essential to get background checks on home-care workers—they may not be kindly grandmoth-ers from Idaho.

Others exploit the elderly in less criminal ways, often target-ing those who live alone: *home shopping channels* offering com-panionship, political action committees offering protection from "gathering political storms," and door to door salesmen offering new roofs.

*What can be done?*

If things haven't gone too far, help the caregiver. Often abuse is triggered by overwork and the solution may be respite care or additional help. Help is also available for alcohol and drug abuse. Maybe a good talk with the caregiver, pointing out that police and prosecutors are beginning to target elder abuse and that these aren't defenses:

* the victim was hard to deal with;

* the victim abused you in the past; or

* the money, down the road, would have been yours, anyway.

But in most cases preventing abuse is best left to the experts. Human relationships are always complicated and abuse is not al-ways a one-way street, not always a black and white affair. Some victims trigger abuse by being too demanding, too sarcastic, too unappreciative. There may be payoffs for the victim, a sense of vindication when the abuser strikes out, and then, on bended knee and with flowers, seeks forgiveness. Adult Protective Services are the folks to contact (if not the police). The national clearing house: 1-800-677-1116. Although state laws differ, often doctors and medical professionals, social and welfare workers, and even bankers, accountants and lawyers may be *required* to report if they know of or suspect physical abuse, neglect or financial exploitation.

### Abuse by Family Members: Protective orders

In most states a battered spouse (not always the wife) can go to court, fill out a simple form, and get a order requiring the aggressor to stay away, even if it means moving out of the house. No need for a lawyer. If the abuser show up, he can be arrested for *violating* the order; they need *not* do anything more in terms of threats or abuse.

### Mentally Impaired Victims

If the victim is mentally impaired emergency *guardianships* can remove the victim from an abusive situation. Emergency *conservatorships* can be sought to freeze assets to protect against financial exploitation.

### Civil commitment

Under most state laws, mentally ill individuals who present a danger to themselves (not eating, threatening suicide) or to others (not careful with fire), can be taken into emergency custody and, after a hearing, committed to a mental hospital for treatment. The length of the commitment and the procedures vary according to state statute. Contact Adult Protective Services.

*Self Abuse: Flying Off to Vegas (where the money stays)*

If suddenly someone begins to waste money, a conservatorship (in some states, "guardianship of the estate" or even, as in Louisiana, a "curatorship") can be sought on an emergency basis. The appointed conservator will take charge of the person's finances—bank accounts, property, stocks. Before that, banks, credit card companies, and financial institutions can be notified.

The rub: what looks like reckless may be sowing one's oats. Say an aging aunt is taking the gardener on weekend trips to Vegas. Unless she no longer has legal capacity or unless he is putting undue pressure on her, she is free to spend her money any way she wants—even if it means the heirs won't be getting any. Let's end this very depressing chapter on a high note, a poem by Edna St. Vincent Millay:

*My candle burns at both ends;*

*It will not last the night;*

*But ah, my foes, and oh, my friends—*

*It gives a lovely light!*

*PART 4*

# *Caring for Others*

_____

# CHAPTER 14

# Caring for Others

In almost one in four homes someone is caring for a physically or mentally disabled relative. A typical caregiver spends about 18 hours a week providing care: doctor visits, managing finances, and hands-on help. Two-thirds work outside the home and, of these, more than half have to make workplace adjustments: coming in late, going part-time, giving up promotions.

If the caregiver works, the employer might be agreeable to flex time. Many corporations now have eldercare programs. Under the Family and Medical Leave Act, companies with more than 50 employees must allow *unpaid* leave to care for sick family members. Working outside the home may make sense even if *all* the earning goes to home care. Getting out of the house is generally a good idea.

It is very hard to appreciate the monetary cost and heartache of caring for elders. All too frequently siblings who are not the caregivers accuse the caregiver of wasting money, of taking advantage, and, when the Will is eventually read, of using undue influence. Families should be encouraged to work things out early-on.

We'll first look at some legal matters that should to addressed and then see if there are financial and support sources that are being overlooked. We'll close raising the constant danger: elder abuse.

*Law Stuff*

Caregivers should be made agents under a *Health Care Power of Attorney* and be given *HIPAA releases* giving them the right to discuss medical conditions with doctors. In the case of mental decline joint checking accounts should be considered to allow the caregiver to pay the bills. Caregivers should be warned against the twin temptations *("It will be mine soon anyway"* and *"I'll borrow some now and pay it back later").* Prosecutors aggressively purse financial abuse of elders. Keeping records is essential not only to keep one clear of the law but also to prevent family fights.

*Financial Stuff*

While Medicare does not pay for home care, some *long term insurance policies* will. Medicare will pay for some medical equipment and does pay almost all of the costs associated with hospice.

Caring for a disabled relative may entitle the caregiver to an additional "dependent" deduction. If the individual is under 65, he or she may qualify for Social Security Disability. The disability (disease, illness, condition) must be one that will last a year or result in death. *Early Alzheimer's* is now listed in the Compassionate Allowance program which means that it will be fast-tracked.

Older folks may be entitled to many benefits: low cost drugs, food stamps, home care aids, and transportation. The National Council on Aging has a slogan: *You Gave, Now Save!"* There are two information resources which tailor their responses to the individual's location, income, veteran status and other factors:

Eldercare Locator 800-677-1116; www.eldercare.gov

BenefitsCheckUp www.benefitscheckup.org

*Practical Stuff*

The well being of the caregiver is critically important in assuring good care. They need support, ideas, and time out. *Support groups*, organized around specific illnesses such as cancer, diabetes, heart disease, arthritis, or Alzheimer's, can be found at Area Council on Aging, or on the Web.

*Adult Day Care* can help. Book clubs, computer training, exercise, music and art, underscore the continuing vibrancy of the individual: life is more than soaps on TV. Alzheimer's patients do better if they have goals to pursue. A friend gives his mother a daily computer problem: "If I'm in London and want to go to Glasgow, what train would I take, how much would it cost, when would it leave, and do they serve tea?" (Of course this is a variation of the old standby, "A train leaves New York going 65 mile per hour . . .")

*Respite care,* at the home or as temporary stays in a nursing home, may be partly covered by insurance and Medicare. Hiring part-time or full-time help is an option. Be cautious. Theft is a worry; so too, abuse.

*Online help.* Updating family and friends, coordinating visits, and seeking help and advice can be made much easier by creating a *private website*. At this writing they are: LotsaHelpingHands; Saturing; and CareZone. Another technical advance that helps is *Skype* which allows caregivers to phone home and see how things are going.

Geriatric Care Managers can help. While there is no licensing required, most come from the helping professions and are quite knowledgeable.

*Scary Stuff: possible abuse*

Is the caregiver often fatigued and irritable? Drinking more or using more drugs? Missing the person's dinner or bath? Getting so upset so as to shove or push? One very good question: *"When was the last time someone visited the patient?"* Isolating the patient is often a sign of abuse.

If you suspect actual abuse, you may have, under the laws of some states, an obligation to report it to Adult Protective Services. If you learned of this in a confidential conversation, unless it suggests future abuse as opposed to what happened in the past, you might have an obligation not to report it.

# CHAPTER 15

# Deciding for Others

*It's 2am. The hospital calls. Your mother has been in a bad accident and is unconscious. Her chances would improve if they amputate her arm. If you were the patient, you would have the amputation. You also believe it would be in her best interests—much better to live. However, you recall her telling you that she would rather be dead than to lose an arm. What do you decide?*

1. Do what you would do if you were the patient;

2. Do what is in Mom's "best interests;"

3. Do what Mom would do (even if it isn't in her own best interests).

What guidance does the law give? What can be done before the situation arises to assure better decisions? And how can one avoid the distortion caused by self-interest?

*The law*

The cardinal principle is that surrogate decision-makers are <u>deciding for the other person, not themselves</u>. Number One is wrong (assuming there are still wrong answers). We want to preserve the disabled individual's autonomy and doing what mom would do (known as substituted judgment) best protects that autonomy; being the captain of one's own ship means that one can run it ashore. If one knows what the person would decide, then go for it; if not, then decide on their "best interests." However one can always manipulate: "Sure, Mom said she would rather die than have an amputation, but she said that when she wasn't actually facing the decision. Who knows what she would say now?"

*Avoiding anguishing decisions*

The more the surrogate knows of the person's desires the better the decision will be. While the specifics cannot be anticipated, general dilemmas can be. *"If your recovery was in doubt, would you want major surgery?"* Don't overlook the financial element—though ethicists decry decision-making based on financial considerations, that is a paramount concern for many (perhaps most) seniors when describing their wishes. Seldom do you hear "I don't want to be seen in public with a prosthesis." Much more common: "I don't want to be a burden/expense/problem to my children." Seldom: "I think the dehumanization of breathing and feeding machines is soul-killing." Common: "I don't see the point in spending money keeping me alive for no purpose."

> *\* If I have to manage your money, how important is it to you that I do so to assure that there will be enough left over for your grandchildren?*

> *\* Should I invest for income or growth?*

*Combating Self-Interest*

> *The parents have fulfilled their retirement dream and moved to a mountain cabin. But they are far from emergency help and the dad has a heart condition. What should the children advise?*

One always has *a dog in the fight*. If the parents move back to the City the children won't have to worry as much or drive as far. This is not to suggest that the surrogate's self-interest is always adverse to that of the other person. Moving back to the City may in fact be in the parents' best interest and their children's happiness is a concern of theirs.

How to factor out self-interest? Some recommend that one thinks of someone they admire and ask, "What would they decide?" This is helpful. Remember your undergraduate philosophy course and Kant recommending universalization of the decision: "Would we have all children try to convince their parents to move back to the city?" Of course law students, who have spent countless hours distinguishing cases, know that how one defines the situation dictates the answer.

Our best advice is to simply *fess up* to your dog. Few children say "It is more convenient for me to have my parents near and, as to their happiness, frankly, my dear, I don't give a damn." Rather their interest will lead them to conclude "They will actually be happier in the City."

Memorize this brilliant quotation from someone most of us never heard of, Albert Dicey, a British jurist:

> "A man's interest gives a bias to his judgment far oftener than it corrupts his heart."

# PART 5

# Disability and Dementia

# CHAPTER 16

# Disability: Signs and Causes

You're not a doctor and, as far as we know, you don't even play one on TV. Still you'll need to know a little medicine, if only to recognize problems and point the way. Some ailments are easy to check and correct: bad meds, hearing loss, and bad lighting. Others are more difficult: depression, alcohol and drug abuse, dementia, unnecessary surgery and rehospitalization.

*Two common errors:* Assuming that the afflictions are inevitable part of aging and that nothing can be done. Second assuming that the behavior is within the person's control and that shouting will improve things.

*Strokes*

*FAST: Face Arms Speech Time*

Common signs of stroke: face and arms go numb, speech becomes slurred. Time is critical. If medical help is quick (less than three hours), long term damage can be avoided. Err on the side of caution. Strokes are common, know *FAST*.

*Insomnia*

Perhaps half of those over 60 suffer from insomnia. It's a serious problem, causing falls, confusion, depression, car wrecks and compromised immune systems. Sleep is an important predictor of how long one lives.

Sleeping pills should be the last choice. People who routinely take them are nearly 5 times as likely to die over a two and a half year period. Even though this study overestimates the risk (folks who routinely take sleeping pills probably are sicker than those who don't), there is little doubt that sleeping pills may not provide the best sleep and may adversely affect memory and coordination.

Best to try other remedies: no caffeine or exercise three hours before bed, gentle activities an hour before (yoga, stretching, slow and deep breathing) and a bedtime routine. Reading law books works wonders.

*Bad Meds*

*One in five* seniors is taking either the wrong dosage or the wrong drugs. Often they are under the care of survival doctors, doctors who *don't talk* with each other (a major problem with our health care system). Drugs they prescribe may interact badly. Pharmacists can help by reviewing a list of all the meds, *including over the counter* and *vitamins*.

Check for side effects. Some meds lead to insomnia and others to depression. And it's dumb for patients to tell their doctors to prescribe some drug they saw on TV—docs know better and usually cheaper options; they went to Med School, not Ad School.

*Hearing Loss*

*Two codgers face off. "What did you call me?"*

*"I called you a liar." The other drops his fists.*

*"Oh, that's OK. I thought you called me a lawyer."*

Hearing loss, affecting about 30% of seniors, leads to isolation, may accelerate dementia and, because the ear plays a role in balance, may lead to falls. A vast majority of folks needing hearing aids don't get them. They are no longer bulky and no longer distort sound. However most are effective only at about six feet and background noise remains a constant problem. Most restaurants respond favorably to "I am hard of hearing. Please turn off the music while I'm here." If not mention of the legal requirement of reasonable accommodations under the Americans with Disabilities Act.

"Hearing loops" hold great promise. Installed in public buildings and theaters they transmit words and music directly to a hearing aid: no background noise. Local initiatives, supported by the Hearing Loss Association of America and the American Academy of Audiology, hope to make them common.

Hearing Aids are pricy ($1,600 to $6,800) and are not covered by Medicare or by most insurance policies. Audiologists may arrange payment terms. In selecting a Medicare HMO, coverage in this area may be important. You can get information on state and federal financial help from the Better Hearing Institute (1-800-Ear-Well). Hear Now (1-800-648-HEAR or 303-695-7797 hearing impaired).

Hearing aids are not "plug and play" but require a lot of individual adjustment. Hearing aid dissatisfaction is widespread but much of the problem may be inability to adjust sound levels, improper hearing aid placement, or even failure to keep the hearing aid cleaned.

*Bad lighting*

Fascinating research suggests that many problems, memory loss, slower reaction time, insomnia, and even depression, are possibly caused by *aging eyes*. The aging eye filters out blue light, affecting circadian rhythm—which has adverse health impacts. The process is too complicated for us to understand, never mind explain, but the bottom line is that older folks should expose themselves to bright sunlight (no more than 20 minutes as the sun damages as well) or bright indoor lighting if they can't get outdoors. Skylights? Extra fluorescent lights?

*Depression*

Depression can lead to suicide (way too common among the elderly). It destroys life's pleasures, both for the victims and their families. About one in seven over 65 suffers depression and, of that number, 70% to 90% go untreated.

> * Folks often resist mental health counselors. However *depression is not a disease of circumstance; it is a disease of chemicals.*

> * Folks think nothing can be done. But 80% of elders will get better with treatment.

> * Folks think that depression is in the control of the individual and can be cured with *"Cheer up Pops"* or *"Damn it, knock it off!"* or *"Don't be silly—you have a lot to live for."*

Professional help is called for.

Things are improving due to new antidepressants that seniors can tolerate better and to more screening for depression. Under the Affordable Care Act depression screening is part of the "Welcome to Medicare" free visit and annual visits thereafter. One shouldn't give up on treatment too early; often to get the right mix of meds takes four or five iterations of treatment.

Be aware that depression is frequently the root cause of what appears to be dementia, and that it is common in the population of seniors. Families should consider the possibility and speak with the senior's medical treatment team.

*Diet*

Sometimes death or incapacity of a loved one, a move to a new location or other disruptions in a senior's life can change eating habits with disastrous results. There is a growing body of research that suggests that a diet rich in Omega-3 fatty acids and antioxidants may slow or delay dementia. So eat more fish, blueberries, broccoli—but don't try to get them in a single dish. That would just be unappetizing.

*Alcoholism, drug addiction, and smoking*

Drug addiction is becoming a major problem, not only because many left their hearts (and common sense) in San Francisco, but also because of addictive prescription drugs. Alcohol abuse, often hidden (vodka being "breathless"), can become a problem as folks can no longer process alcohol as they did in their youth. What they are "used to" becomes dangerous. Red wine? The National Institute of Alcohol Abuse and Alcoholism recommends not more than one drink a day. Smoking? "What the hell, why quit now? I'll wait until I burn the house down."

Groups and agencies offer treatments, including "interventions." If a doctor recommends inpatient treatment Medicare may cover most of the cost.

*Memory Loss and Alzheimer's*

"I don't remember being absent minded." Everyone loses some memory. (Have we said that before?) Short-term memory goes first: "What did I have for breakfast yesterday?" Names fade quickly; they are arbitrary—our dentist could have been named Sally instead of Carol (she's actually named Martha, but that's another story). Memory loss is irksome and frightening: is this the first sign? It does *not* inevitably lead to dementia or senility. It does *not* necessarily get worse. However dementia is a very serious matter and we devote the next chapter to it.

*Surgery*

Benefits and risks. Are there alternatives? How long the rehab? What the quality of life? If nothing is done, what will happen? How many have had the surgery and lived? And died?

Doctors may put a happy face on things, perhaps focusing on something they can cure to avoid talking about what they can't. Trained to "do something," they may want to try something heroic. There are financial aspects. There have been confirmed reports of unnecessary and even dangerous cardiac treatments in some hospitals (always seek a second opinion even if you love your doc). Few doctors consciously run up the bill but *a person's interest far oftener distorts his judgment than corrupts his heart.*

As for patients and family, good news will jump out while bad news will be overlooked or explained away.

Why the concern over late-life surgeries? A 2008 study of almost two million Medicare patients found that nearly *one in three* had surgery the last year of their life, *one in five* the last month of their life, and *one in ten in the last week of life.* No doubt the numbers are skewed as they do not reflect how many folks had surgery and lived. Still, they give one pause.

*Hospitalization*

Coming home isn't the end of worries. Patients are quite vulnerable and need all the support they can get. Studies indicate that aging and dementia may be accelerated by hospital stays. There is an alarming rate of readmission, frequently with medical problems other than those that led to the original hospitalization. A relative or friend, not the patient, should insist on understanding what needs to be done to prevent relapse. Often this will involve several medications and several doctors. Expert advice is available. Most hospitals have social workers who can make recommendations. Professional Geriatric Care Managers can also be of help. Usually nurses or social workers they can coordinate medical care. Call their Association at 520-881-8008 or look online at www.findacaremanager.org.

Now you know as much as House and he *does* play one on TV.

*CHAPTER 17*

# Dementia

Dementia causes undue hardship. A guardianship may be required and perhaps a nursing home. We address those topics in the next chapters. Here we hook at immediate problems facing the family: getting an evaluation, executing the needed documents, stopping the individual from driving and dealing with the constant fear of wandering off. Tips on home care were offered in previous chapters.

The National Institute on Aging estimates that 5% of those 65 to 74 suffer from dementia and the percentage grows quickly after that, reaching 50% for folks over 85. Many fear that Alzheimer's is genetic. While it may be, autopsies disclose that close to half of those who were thought to have Alzheimer's actually did not.

If the person remembers forgetting, the forgotten name and misplaced keys are likely normal. There is more to worry about when the someone forgets that they have forgotten. Missed appointments, memory lapses that interfere with daily living, inability to find the way home from the grocery store—spell trouble.

*Push early evaluation.* Memory loss is often caused by correctable conditions: bad medicine interactions, alcohol, drugs or depression, hearing loss and diabetics. While most forms of dementia cannot be cured, there are drugs to control some symptoms and families can set in place procedures to deal more effectively with decline.

The patient and the family may resist evaluation. There will be a lot of denial and excuses ("It was the Holidays, no wonder she forgot all her appointments.") Often gentle third party urging is helpful.

Getting the *legal documents* in order becomes a priority. The individual must have *legal capacity*, (the ability to recognize alternatives, to weigh pros and cons, and to project into the future). To check on someone's mental capacity test their "executive function". Ask questions like, "If you wanted to take a trip to Europe, how would you go about it?" If the answer touches upon travel agents and airline tickets, fine. Be concerned with "I don't know" or "I'd rather go to Timbuktu."

*Wandering off* is a constant fear. Call the police and *tell them that the person has dementia* (otherwise they won't take the matter seriously). The *"Safe Return Program"* can help. For a one-time registration fee, a bracelet and clothing tags will be provided with a toll free number. If someone finds the person, they call the number and the operator will then contact the caregiver listed in the database. This service is available 24 hours a day. Soon there will be shoes which transmitters embedded that will alert your phone if the person wanders off. Unlike bracelets and tags, these transmitters cannot be removed. There is even an "app" for smartphones that will alert one's computer or cell phone where the individual is. For more information, call the Alzheimer's Association at 1-800-272-3900 (hearing impaired 312-335-8882).

*Driving.* Forgetting where you are going kills. We have elderly clients with a history of accidents—none of which was their "fault." Multiple accidents is an indication that something is wrong, even if it is the other driver who got the citation. One client had three different left-turn accidents, in which she ever-so-slowly hit someone turning in front of her. In each case the turning driver was cited; her accident-prone danger was removed only by taking away her vehicle.

It is not enough, however, to suspend the license, impound or disable the vehicle. Driving is a key element of our modern American lifestyle. Few cities have adequate or affordable public transportation, and some alternative must be provided.

We highly recommend "The 36-Hour Day" by Nancy L. Mace and Dr. Peter V. Rabins—it contains invaluable advice, information and comfort for anyone with a family member suffering from dementia. And there are blogs, such as *Alzheimer's Reading Room.*

There will come a time, and with Alzheimer's it is almost a certainty, when home care is no longer an option. When will be that time? When wandering off becomes routine, when the person hates one of the family, or when the caregiver is on the edge of physical violence.

*Start looking early* for independent living arrangements, assisted living facilities or nursing homes now. Last minute decisions are not the best. The longer one looks the better the options. Area Council, hospice nurses, know what is available.

*There is no need to break the bank.* All the person needs is a clean place to live, good food, and one that will prevent wandering off. Independent or assisted living facilities may provide all the required support for a senior who does not require extensive medical care and supervision. If the move to such a facility is made early, it may help delay or even prevent a move to a higher level of care.

# CHAPTER 18

# Nursing Homes and Geriatric Care Managers

In many ways a good nursing home care is better than home care. While residents lose privacy and sense of home, nursing homes provide better medical treatment with nurses, certified nursing assistants and, sometimes, physicians on staff. Most provide exercise programs, craft classes, and field trips. And there's a lot to be said for hanging out with folks your own age talking Ed Sullivan, the Great Depression, and Andrews Sisters. Many fear dying in a nursing home. It's always possible to return home at the time of one's last illness and receive hospice care.

The major mistake is waiting too long before considering this option; too many are rushed into a nursing home when they are released from the hospital, after a fall, a major accident, a heart attack, or when the family just can't take it anymore. One task is to decide what level of care is needed.

*Hospice care:* This is end-of-life care, often at home, usually (but not always) paid by Medicare.

*Skilled-nursing home care:* This usually follows hospitalization for the short term; it is expected that the patient will return home. Some of the costs are picked up by Medicare—if the patient is deemed to have *rehabilitative potential* but under a new policy it will pay even if this is not so as in the cases of Alzheimer's, MS and Parkinson's.

*Custodial care:* It is expected that the patient will *not* return home *unless* it is to die at home. The costs of custodial care are *not* covered by Medicare.

There are a host of alternatives to nursing homes, depending on the level of disability, including subsidized senior housing, independent living and assisted living facilities, and Continuing Care Retirement Communities (CCRCs). Good advice is crucial.

*Geriatric Care Managers,* trained in gerontology, social work, nursing, or counseling, provide a bundle of services, from financial and physical assessments to recommendations of living arrangements. They can also help with long-distance arrangements, and be surrogate eyes and ears to monitor future care. The field is unregulated but there is a National Association of Professional Geriatric Care Managers. Ask about training, scope of services, and letters of recommendation. Call the Association at 520-881-8008 or look online at www.findacaremanager.org.

*Selecting a Nursing Home*

Some nursing homes are great; others, both figuratively and literally, stink. Remember, "It's the location, location, location!"

*Who to talk to?* Hospital discharge planners, social workers, doctors, clergy and volunteers who help the elderly. Every community has a Long-Term Care Ombudsman who visits nursing homes and takes complaints. They cannot recommend homes but can answer questions about complaints and survey results. Other re-sources:

* National Citizen's Coalition for Nursing Home Reform which publishes "Nursing Homes: Getting Good Care There"

* Medicare maintains a database of nursing homes and their past performances. www.medicare.gov/NHCompare/. It has an excellent checklist.

*Visit* at least two (we can't see without contrasts) and visit each several times, at different times of day. *Don't make appointments; just show up.*

*Staff.* Adequate to give individual attention or overworked? How does the staff treat the residents? *Turnover:* 30% per year is okay; 50% spells trouble.

*Mealtimes.* Do residents socialize? Residents needing help should be integrated with other residents rather than eating alone.

*Resident rooms.* Personalized or institutionalized?

*Residents.* Reasonably well groomed, clean, and dressed?

*Restraints and bedsores.* Too many residents physically or medically restrained and too many bedsores spell trouble.

*Activities.* Speaking of activities, what is the policy concerning resident *sex*?

*Location.* The more the family can visit, the better. Nurses will pay more attention to residents who do not appear to be abandoned.

Nursing homes with Medicaid patients are routinely inspected and hence might have an edge.

*Patients' Rights*

The federal Nursing Home Reform Act (NHRA) applies to any home that has Medicare or Medicaid patients (a majority of such homes). The NHRA requires that a patient Bill of Rights be given to residents and their families. The most important rights include an individualized treatment plan; to see all of one's clinical records; to complain and be free from reprisal; to send and receive uncensored mail and to make private calls; to refuse treatment; and *not* to be physically or chemically restrained except to prevent physical harm, and then only upon instruction of a doctor.

We cannot stress the importance of the right not to be restrained except under very limited circumstances. In some nursing homes, patients are routinely tied to their chairs. By their arms. Considerable medical evidence indicates that this actually *increases* the incidence of injuries, as patients struggle against restraints, get caught in the restraining devices, or are simply left unattended. For more of this problem visit the website of "Untie the Elderly," a project of the Kendal Corporation, a faith-based organization active in the Northeast.

*Abuse*

Visit often. Adopt the "cookies and thorns" approach. Bring cookies to the facility's staff, and think of your job as being a constant thorn in the facility's side. You have the right to inspect medical charts. The nursing home has 24 hours to make them available.

*Law and Costs*

If the patient has mental capacity, they can check themselves in. If not, there might be a hassle. Best to have a *Health Care Power of Attorney* giving the agent that power and, even then, some states require that a *guardianship* be obtained.

As to costs, nursing homes are quite expensive, perhaps $170,000 a year. Medicare doesn't not pay. The costs are covered by Medicaid, the program for low income folks. It is possible for some middle income folks to "spend down" so as to make themselves eligible for Medicaid but it is very tricky; one needs a specialist.

# CHAPTER 19

# Guardianships

*Guardianships* or *conservatorships,* are serious. The "ward" forfeits some or all of their adulthood in the sense that some or all of their right to make their own decisions is taken from them. When should they be considered?

* Where individuals lack the mental capacity to manage their finances.

* Where individuals lack the mental capacity to make health decisions and their health is suffering badly, either because they refuse needed treatment or to move into a nursing home to get needed treatment.

* Where a disabled individual is being financially or physically abused by their caregiver.

A friend or relative can file the petition. They should be reluctant to do so and should be aware of their own self-interest— that the guardianship will make things easier for them or will preserve money that they will eventually get. Again, a person's interest far more often distorts their judgment than corrupts their heart.

*Bad decisions don't necessarily mean lack of capacity.* If the person retains mental capacity, roughly the ability to see and weigh alternatives and project into the future, they have the right to do what they will: refuse life saving treatment, get a nose ring, or fly off to Vegas wasting the kids' inheritance.

*Mental capacity is not an all or nothing thing.* A person can lack the ability to manage finances but be perfectly competent to decide where to live and what medical treatment to have. Capacity may be variable over *time* (seniors can be more alert in the morning than in the evening), *setting* (dressing up and going to the lawyer's office may temporarily improve the senior's ability to focus) and *topic* (some seniors may be able to give extensive histories and directions for their cat but not identify all of their children by name). Even these categories are too broad and some courts will narrow a guardianship still further, say over the person's stocks and bonds but not management of his Social Security check and day-to-day finances.

## Terminology

Some states use "guardian" to identify a court-appointed person who makes medical decisions and "conservator" as the name for one appointed to handle finances. Some states use "guardian" to mean both, and some use "conservator" to cover both. Some states use "guardian" for wards who are minors and "conservator" for adult wards. In other words, watch your words.

## Expenses

In almost all cases a lawyer will be needed by the petitioner and thus the costs may be substantial (in the neighborhood of $500 to $3,000, perhaps—or more, in localities with higher legal costs).

In many states (but not all), a separate lawyer for the ward and/or a court investigator will also be appointed, incurring an additional cost.

*Hearing*

The court hearing comes quickly, usually in a few weeks (and emergency situations can make the system respond even more quickly). The proposed ward usually will not be present unless the matter is contested, though he or she has the right to attend. Some judges will even go to the person's home to conduct the hearing.

The individual has a right to an attorney (to resist the guardianship or to object to a particular person as guardian) and, in some states, if the individual has not selected a lawyer, one will automatically be appointed and will be paid by from the ward's estate (or, if the ward is indigent, by the court). In some states, before the hearing, the court will appoint a Court Visitor or Investigator.

*Routine guardianships* are usually quick. A short court hearing will be held with the person seeking the guardianship, his lawyer, and the lawyer for the ward (usually court appointed) meeting to see if all is in order.

*Contested guardianships* are more like trials. They are contested if the individual insists they are mentally competent, if relatives are in a fight over ending life-sustaining treatment, or if there is a fight over who should be the guardian.

At the hearing, the judge (in some states, the jury, if requested by the ward) first decides whether the individual is competent; if competent, everyone goes home. If the decision goes against the individual, two questions remain: what kind of guardian should be appointed (*financial* or *personal*), and who should be the guardian?

## Who should be the guardian?

Usually it will be the petitioner. However in the case of large or complicated financial estates, it might be a bank or trust company, or a private professional fiduciary. If no family member can or wishes to serve, the guardian can be a social service agency which will usually charge a fee. Public Guardians are available in some states for individuals who have no one else. Private fiduciaries are available in most communities. Check if they are licensed (some states require it) and if they are bonded. There is a national certification for professional fiduciaries; it may not be required, but it might provide some comfort to know that the guardian is familiar with best practices and national trends. For more information about the national certification standards, visit http://www.guardianshipcert.org/.

Typically, family members serve without charge (though that is not necessarily the case). Expenses (lawyers, accountants, travel) can be charged against the ward's estate. Institutional guardians charge for their services, usually on an hourly-fee basis or for a percentage of the estate assets.

## Court-Appointed Guardians: Powers and Duties

Guardians are given a court document to show to banks, doctors, and others (usually called "Letters of Guardianship" or something similar) and will probably be required to report back to the court yearly or even more frequently. They should keep records as to expenditures. The big danger: *co-mingling funds.* People with the very best of intentions ("I'll put it back next week" or "It's easier to handle that way" or "We've always operated as a family") get into big trouble.

# PART 6

# Finances, Medical Care, and Housing

# CHAPTER 20

# Social Security, Pensions, and IRAs

*Wives make the little decisions, what to have for dinner, when to go on vacation, what house to buy, and where the kids go to college. Husbands make the big decisions, like whether there should be a playoff system in college football.*

If one spouse (often, especially among seniors who grew up in a different cultural milieu from today's, the husband) handles all the finances the other should get up to speed. Community colleges might offer courses, and one good website is WIFE (Women's Institute for Financial Education).

## Social Security

Social Security is the child of the Great Depression, folks selling apples, losing farms, and Franklin Roosevelt (*"The only thing we have to fear is Fear itself."*) It's financed by a payroll tax on the first $110,100 of earnings.

Whether it is going broke and how to fix Social Security are beyond our scope (thankfully). We note two things. First, the cost of caring for the elderly will not go away. Shift it from Social Security and it falls on sons and daughters, or government welfare benefits. Second, Social Security has done wonderful things.

* The poverty rate among folks over 65 is no longer 70% as it was before Social Security; it is now 12% (about the same rate for people under 65).

* Of the more than 48 million currently receiving benefits, one-fourth are the families of workers who have died or become disabled.

* For over half of Social Security retirees, the program provides the majority of their income. For about a quarter of them, Social Security represents more than 90% of their income.

* Its administrative costs are about *1%* (compared to around 15% for private pension plans).

*Insurance benefits*

*Social Security is more than a retirement program.* If an insured worker (and most everyone is) becomes permanently disabled *disability* benefits are available. *Life insurance*-like benefits are also provided in the form of payments to survivors upon the death of a covered worker.

*Retirement benefits*

To be *eligible* for retirement benefits one must have paid into the program for 40 calendar quarters. *Folks should try to get the 40 quarters*; while they may not get a big retirement check for the minimum investment, they will be eligible for Medicare (otherwise it costs a bundle). It is also possible for younger people to be covered with shorter work histories; this is important for the disability part of the Social Security benefit.

The longer one has worked and the higher one's earnings, the larger the monthly check. The system slightly favors lower end earners; workers who have earned half the national average will receive about 56% of their average salary, average workers about 42%, while folks at the high end typically get about 28%. For a comfortable retirement folks need about 70% or 80% of pre-retirement income, not 56%, 42%, or 28%. It is a *serious mistake* to think that Social Security will maintain one's standard of living. In 2012, the average monthly payment for a retired individual was $1,229 and, for a couple both receiving benefits, $1,994.

How does Social Security compute your benefits? Like this:

*A train leaves New York going West at 60 mph. Two hours and 13 minutes later, another train leaves Los Angeles, going East at 62 mph. What is the capital of Nova Scotia?*

The basic idea is to determine one's *average monthly salary* and then give you a *percentage of that figure*. It assumes a work history of *35 years*: total earning are spread out over this period.

*Family benefits*

Family members might entitled to benefits: spouses, children and even dependent grandchildren and dependent parents. Definitely worth a call to Social Security. *Divorcees* who were married *at least ten years and have not remarried until after age 60* are entitled to a benefit equal to (usually) one-half of the retiree's retirement amount. The divorcee's benefits are usually available at their age 62, or younger if providing care for a dependent minor.

*Early, Late, and Full Retirement*

At "full retirement age" one receives full retirement amount, called the Primary Insurance Amount. Full retirement age is slowly going up; for folks born about 1954 it goes up two months every year until 1959 when full retirement age will be 67.

*Early Retirement.* At *62* (that age is not going up, though the percentage reduction from normal retirement benefits is) one can retire. Should one? There are a host of factors such as health and other sources of income. Three things to consider. *One won't be eligible for Medicare* until 65 regardless of retirement status and, to bridge the gap, one can continue employer's health insurance but must pay the premium. If one continues working, after about $14,000, the social security benefit will be reduced $1 for every $2 earned. Finally there will be a *permanent* reduction of *25% to 30%* in monthly benefits.

Some private pension plans have what is known as an *integration of benefits* clause which operates to *reduce pension payments* in light of what one receives from Social Security. Depending on the rate of reduction, it might be well to delay taking Social Security as long as possible.

On the other hand if the retiree has a *child under 18* or *a spouse over 62, they can begin* drawing benefits which may increase the family's take by as much as 150% to 180%.

*Late retirement.* At 70 checks may be as much as 32% higher (and one is still eligible for Medicare at 65). After the age of 70, there will be no further increase in benefits—virtue finally then becoming its own reward.

*Taxes on benefits*

If there is *no* income other than Social Security, *none* of it is taxed. However if one has income over a threshold amount (currently $25,000 for a single taxpayer or $32,000 for a married couple) up to 50% of Social Security payments may be counted as income. You can request Social Security to withhold federal taxes for you. However, it cannot withhold state taxes.

*Pensions*

*Taxes: "Deduct now, pay later."*

Most money from retirement pensions is taxed as regular income: money going in was deductible from income and hence not taxed. Compare money put in a *savings account*. As these were *post tax* dollars, when taken out, they do *not* constitute income. This is why, generally speaking, it is tax-wise to take money out of savings rather than retirement accounts.

*Basic Plans*

*Defined Benefit Plans.* Retirement payments are based on a percentage of earnings (usually the average of the last three to five years). The percentage goes up yearly, say 2% per year. Work 30 years the retirement will 60% of the average earnings over the last few years.

*Defined Contribution Plans.* Contributions are put in a retirement account and invested. In a defined *contribution* plan, the employee takes the risk of market variations; in a defined *benefit* plan, the employer takes the risk.

*401(k) Plans.* Similar to defined contribution plans, but they give the employee somewhat more flexibility as there are no fixed contributions. The employer may match an employee's contributions up to a certain amount. 401(k) Plans can be risky. First, they depend on how well the investments do, and second, they are not insured. On the other hand, depending on the market, they can do much better than defined benefit plans.

*Contributions and Vesting*

Workers are entitled to get back *all* of their own contributions to their retirement no matter what, laid off, fired or quit. However they are *not* be entitled to the *employer's* contribution until they *vest*. Most vest after *five* years, but this varies widely: some vest in a month, some in seven years (the maximum length under federal tax law).

Some employers fire folks shortly before their retirement rights vest or, in the alternative, make their jobs so miserable that they quit. This is known as a "constructive discharge." Often there will be legal recourse.

*Decisions at Retirement: Cashing Out and Annuities*

*Cashing out.* Unless done correctly the entire amount cashed out will be *current* income. Big taxes. Money rolled over to an IRA is not taxed until it comes out. The retirement plan might offer an annuity option, in which an insurance company offers to make monthly payments at a fixed amount for the life of the retiree (or, sometimes, for a period of years). The problem with putting all the money in an annuity is that one won't be able to get at it in the case of emergencies or leave it to children. IRAs are good for that.

*Joint and survivors' annuities.* Under federal law, *married* individuals *must* elect a joint and survivor's annuity, with the survivor getting at least 50%. A single life annuity (one leaving nothing to the spouse), is possible *only* if the spouse agrees in writing. A *single life annuity*, which will pay the highest monthly payments, makes sense *if* the spouse has adequate retirement income. As a way of passing on wealth, it may be possible to make one's children the beneficiaries.

Pension troubles

*Divorce.* The worth of the pension will have to be divided—and this gets complicated.

*Forgotten pensions.* Old tax forms will give the employer's tax number and perhaps the number of the retirement plan. For a fee the IRS will provide a copy. With these numbers, perhaps the Pension Benefit Guaranty Corporation can help (1-800-400-PBGC). www.pbgc.gov.

*IRAs*

As money going into the IRA was a deduction from current income it will be taxed as regular income when it is withdrawn. The interest earned on the account is not taxed *until* it is withdrawn. This is why IRAs are generally the last cookie jar: money withdrawn from saving accounts is not taxed. However, beginning in the year after one turns 70½, there are mandatory withdrawals.

*Roth IRAs* are better than a regular IRA when it comes time to get money out. First, there is no 70½ rule: no need to take any out for the owner's lifetime. Second, all the money you take out of it (after it has been around for five years, that is), *including* the amount it earned in interest, is tax free. This is because the money put into the Roth IRA was not deductible at the time. It is possible to convert a regular IRA into a Roth IRA. This may make sense although it will trigger a big tax bill.

As to investment, buy low and sell high. *Professional financial planners* work on a *set or hourly fee* and not on a commission which might skew their advice. But they might lack the needed expertise when it comes to stocks, annuities, and other investments. *Certified Financial Planners* (CFP) will have taken a comprehensive course of study and completed a very difficult set of examinations. *Insurance agents, stock brokers, bank advisors* have both expertise (good) and a dog in the fight (bad).

Of course, as John Kenneth Galbraith has said, *"The only function of economic forecasting is to make astrology look good."*

# Reverse Mortgages and Safety Nets: SSDI, SSI, Medicaid

*Beware aging actor offering free CDs!*

*Reverse Mortgages*

Folks considering a reserve mortgage should contact the federal government's *Home Equity Conversion Mortgage Program*, the principal, and most principled, of the reverse mortgage offerings. Borrowers complete a free counseling program (some of the counselors charge, but usually only after a relatively wealthy applicant decides to proceed with the reverse mortgage). Many are shown how to better arrange their finances without going through the reverse mortgage—and that's a sign that the program is more interested in good results than in closings. There are scams out there.

Lenders pay either a lump sum or a monthly amount and the loan does not have to be repaid until one moves or dies. The money is not taxed and doesn't impact Social Security, Medicare or Medicaid. Title stays in the owner's name. There are no income limits and any kind of house can qualify, from mansion to house trailer, with the exceptions being cooperative apartments and newly-built (less than a year) dwellings.

The loans are costly. First, there are substantial closing costs and fees which are generally hidden. Second, the borrower is paying interest on interest: interest that is not paid as the homeowner continues to live at home is added to the outstanding balance each month.

Interest rates will vary and are usually adjustable rather than fixed. One can terminate the loan early and repay it at that time. At death if the surviving spouse is on the deed the loan payments will continue. If not, the house goes to the heirs with the mortgage lien attached. Heirs can either pay off the loan and keep the house, or allow it to be sold. If the selling price exceeds the amount due under the loan, that money goes to the heirs.

Borrowers must continue to live in the house at least half time. Reverse mortgages, due to the paperwork and costs, aren't a good idea for anyone planning to move. The AARP website has a wealth of information, from eligibility, basics, and lenders, to options and loan calculations.

### SSDI (Social Security Disability)

Social Security provides a monthly disability benefit. The disability must prevent "any substantial gainful activity" (not just the job held by the applicant before the injury) and it must be one that will last for a year or until death.

The cases often involve tricky medical issues. Social Security pays the lawyer if there is one—but by withholding the fee from the monthly benefit check. The average payment for a disabled married worker, with children, is around $2,000 per month.

## SSI (Supplemental Security Income)

This welfare program run by Social Security pays monthly checks to the *elderly*, the blind, and to people with disabilities who don't have much income or property. Recipients of SSI usually get food stamps and Medicaid.

The payments are pretty low (a maximum of about $700/month, with some variation by state) and the property and income restrictions are fairly severe.

## Medicaid and Medicaid Planning

Not to be confused with *Medicare* (the program for folks over 65), *Medicaid* is a federal program for low income folks adminis-tered by the states. There are income and property limitations but no age limitations. It provides a full range of medical services, including *long term* care.

Long term nursing care is extremely expensive. There is a new legal specialty, *Medicaid (or Long-Term Care) Planning*, de-signed to make folks eligible for Medicaid while protecting the family's assets. It is very complicated with regulations changing as we speak. Long-term care insurance is an alternative but, with most seniors, probably will be wildly expensive. Still, the average age of new long-term care insurance buyers had hovered just un-der age 70 for decades, and recently dipped just below 60.

## Section 8 Housing

A rent subsidy program for folks 62 or older who will pay a certain percentage of their income in rent with the federal gov-ernment picking up the difference. Although many Americans hold onto images of government housing being clustered into substand-ard buildings in dangerous neighborhoods, Section 8 subsidies today may be available for rental units pretty much anywhere in town.

*Other Sources*

Other benefits may be available: low cost drugs, food stamps, home care aids, and transportation. There are two information resources which tailor their responses to the individual's location, income, veteran status and other factors. Take a look at Eldercare Locator (www.eldercare.gov) or BenefitsCheckUp (www.benefits checkup.org) for information on what other benefits are available.

# CHAPTER 22

# Medicare

Medicare assures that families will not go bankrupt paying astronomical hospital or doctor's bills. It is quite complicated and the subject of fierce political debate. Here a quick overview of its various components. Perhaps the first important thing to know is what it *doesn't* cover:

*Glasses, hearing aids, over the counter drugs, co-payments, insurance premiums, and long-term care.*

These add up quickly. Putting aside long-term care, a recent study of folks over 70 indicated average expenditures over $7,000 per year. *What it does cover?*

*Medicare Part A: Hospitals*

Covers most hospital costs, some skilled nursing, some home care costs, and, importantly, most hospice care. *Medicare and You* explains the complexities. *Sixty five* is the magic age (apply a few months before) and one must be *eligible* for Social Security (no need to be drawing retirement benefits). Spouses, widows, and widowers of an eligible member are eligible at their own age 65, as are ex-spouses, if married for more than ten years and not re-married. If not eligible for Medicare you can buy in; it costs over $450 per month. (It will be less if you have at least 30 Social Security quarters.) It is free for covered participants; paid for it by their payroll taxes.

*Medicare Part B: Doctor Visits*

Medicare Part B covers doctor visits and helps with outpatient hospital services (including emergency room visits), ambulances, diagnostic tests, laboratory services, some preventive care such as mammography and Pap smear, outpatient therapy services, durable medical equipment and supplies, and a variety of other services. It also picks up some home health care services. There is a yearly deductible, currently $155 and 20% of additional charges.

One is automatically enrolled in Part B when one signs up for Medicare unless one *opts out,* (having other insurance covering the same benefits). There is almost no good reason to ever opt out of Part B. A monthly premium is taken from one's Social Security check, about $100 per month or higher for high income folks. It is a great value, the premium being set at 25% of the cost of the care provided to all participants— in other words, comparable coverage in the private market would cost about four times as much.

Part B does *not* cover prescriptions, dental, hearing, or vision services.

Medicare Part D: Prescriptions

This covers outpatient drugs. Medicare recommends signing up for Part D when turning 65; the longer the delay, the higher the premiums. Private insurers provide the benefits and the premiums and extent of coverage varies. There will be yearly deductibles and co-pays. To get through the maze visit www.medicare.gov, check out the Prescription Drug Plan Finder. Enter specific needs (including the actual prescriptions you are seeking coverage for) and it will calculate "Estimated Annual Cost," and then give two or three plans to choose. Note that each plan is permitted to have its own "formulary." That means that different plans will work better for different patients, and the costs will vary, often wildly, for each patient.

*Medigap Policies: Dental, Glasses, Hearing Aids*

*do not cover*

Neither Parts A nor B cover dental care or dentures, cosmetic surgery, routine foot care, hearing aids, eye exams, or glasses. Except for certain limited cases in Canada and Mexico, Medicare does not pay for treatment outside of the United States; those who travel regularly or plan a particular trip should get foreign medical coverage before leaving the U.S.

Medigap policies cover some of these gaps and provide coverage for some of the co-payments and deductibles in the Medicare programs. Some even cover prescription drugs. In order to simplify purchasing and make it possible to make meaningful comparisons, the federal government restricts Medigap insurance plans to one of 13 basic policy benefit lists.

*The HMO Alternative*

There are two basic options:

1. Staying in Medicare program: Part A and B, a drug policy under Part D, and a possible Medigap policy. *Or*

2. Joining a Medicare HMO.

Health Maintenance Organizations, run by various insurance companies, can provide most of the benefits covered by the various Medicare programs. The idea was to get private industry involved to drive down Medicare costs. This is currently controversial, the allegation being that HMOs take the healthy seniors while leaving the sick, and more expensive, to the traditional program. Expect changes as Congress looks at the entire Medicare program.

Part A and Part B benefits are assigned to the HMO. One big advantage of staying with the basic Medicare program is the freedom to choose your own physicians and other health care providers. Many HMOs, though not all, limit choices.

Seniors, faced with these confusing choices, need help. The best resource is the Area Agency on Aging. Every region of the country has one and can be found at Administration on Aging's website at www.aoa.gov.

One final note: two big items are not covered by Medicare: long-term nursing care and over the counter drugs.

*PART 7*

# Estate Planning

# CHAPTER 23

# Estate Planning: An Overview

*"Estate Planning" smacks of an English novel, anxious heirs sitting before a roaring fireplace, and an elderly lawyer fumbling papers. Did Old Codger really mean to cut out his first son in favor of his new, young wife? Did the new wife forge his signature? 400 pages to go!*

Everyone should have an Estate Plan; it will save them and their families money, time, and heartbreak. Estate plans consist of *two* kinds of documents:

1. Those dealing with incapacity and

2. Those dealing with passing on property.

*Time's winged chariot is hurrying near.* Once an individual loses legal competence, the unplanned option to deal with health and financial matters will be a guardianship. That means confusion, expense, and lawyer visits. And if one dies without a Will, property will pass under the state's intestacy law which may not be the best for the family.

*Preparing for mental disability*

As to handling *health matters* we will recommend a *Living Will* and, more importantly, a *Health Care Power of Attorney*. Note that different states favor different terminology (so a Health Care Power of Attorney might be called an *Appointment of Health Surrogate*). As to *financial affairs*, if most of the income is from Social Security and retirement checks, a special form of *joint account* can be set up. *Powers of Attorney* are *essential*—also dangerous and inadequate. For larger estates consider a *Trust* (or *Living Trust*); the trustee will make the financial decisions if you become unable to do so.

*Passing property*

Most write a *Will*. *Living Trusts* can be used to pass property as can *life-time gifts, joint ownership (at least some kinds), beneficiary designations* and *life insurance*. Gifts and bequests to minors and relatives with special needs trigger problems.

We describe all of these options in the following chapters. Here a few essential points.

\* Many of your clients will already have an estate plan. Urge them to *update* it *every five years* or so—kids graduate, grandchildren arrive, lotteries won. Don't overlook *IRAs* and *401k* plans—and check the beneficiary designations.

\* Many hold their home and stocks and bonds in *joint tenancy* as a way of passing property. *Joint tenancy* usually includes (or implies) the additional notion of *with right of survivorship*. *Joint tenancy with right of survivorship* is a kind of legal tontine—the last surviving joint tenant owns the entire property. Joint ownership through *tenancy in common*, the other principal method for a group of people to own property together, means that at death each co-owner's share remains in his or her estate.

\* Making gifts of appreciated assets, (perhaps the family home or long-time stock holdings), may cause negative income tax consequences. It may make more tax sense to hold those assets until death and let them pass to offspring by Will—or Trust—in order to minimize capital gains taxes. This is really boring and we will explain it more in another chapter.

\* No such thing as a free lunch? Then imagine how often those free estate planning dinners turn out favorably. Living Trusts (and, often, annuities) are sold at them; most buyers don't need them and often get flawed ones. Lawyers are better and cheaper.

\* *Estate taxes* are probably not an issue. A tiny minority of clients (those worth more than about $5 million, or couples worth double that amount) will face any possibility of federal estate tax liability—though they may aspire to have a larger estate and insist on planning for the remote possibility. A handful of states impose estate taxes on smaller estates, but still only a minority of clients will need to be very concerned about estate taxes. Avoiding probate, incidentally, doesn't mean avoiding estate taxes; most of the property that was taken out of the estate to avoid probate gets pulled back in for estate tax purposes—if that is important in individual cases.

\* As to *avoiding probate,* the basic idea is to get rid of your stuff. We'll discuss the ways. However, avoiding probate is much less of an issue than it was in the time of Charles Dickens' *Bleak House.* And it can be overdone. Jay Leno was talking to folks mailing their 1040s as the clock neared midnight on April 15. One explained,

> *"The IRS will get nothing from me! I quit my job, got rid of my house, my car, and spent all my savings!"*

> *"Wow! You sure did show them!"*

*CHAPTER 24*

# **Wills**

---

*As to the meaning of life, lawyers don't have a clue, but when it comes to dealing with the decedent's stuff, they're crackerjacks!*

"Wow, I can't believe this, I was going to leave money to that jerk, cousin Joe!" Times change, finances improve; charities offend; children, sometimes, move out—or back in. *Update Wills at least every 5 years.*

Everyone needs a Will. Even if one has a Living Trust it is important to plan for what happens to the stuff that isn't "in" the Trust. State intestacy laws represent the legislature's best guess as to how most people would want their property distributed (generally first to their spouse, then to their children, and then to more distant relatives). The problems:

* Many states provide that at the death of one spouse, only a portion of his or her property goes to the surviving spouse, the rest to the children. Some may want everything to go to their spouse. If the children are minors, or receive public benefits, or are spendthrifts, there may be trouble if they get cash outright.

  * Intestacy laws treat everyone the same. Children take in equal shares even though some may be younger, some may have special problems, some may have already gotten a college education and some may be brats or spend-thrifts.

  * Friends, distant relatives, or favorite charities receive squat.

  * Parents can't nominate guardians for the *minor* children.

  * *If a business is involved, it will be shipwrecked.*

  * Estate taxes may take a large portion and probate will not be avoided.

A good estate plan can avoid all of these problems. We'll show you how.

*Issues to Consider in Making a Will*

  *\*Gifts to minors or relatives with special needs*

  Minors lack legal capacity and, when they get it, may lack good sense. Relatives with special needs might also lack legal capacity and, if they are receiving public benefits, gifts might make them ineligible. *Trusts are the way to go.* They allow one to delay, stage and condition gifts. When properly drafted, Trusts allow the individual to continue to receive public benefits while the assets and income can be used to meet supplemental needs.

  * *What if a beneficiary dies first?*

  Assume three adult children and the testator wants to divide the estate into three equal shares. What happens if one dies before the testator? Should the surviving two divide the estate or should the child of the deceased child take the one-third? What if there are two such children? Lawyers spend untold hours imagining

unusual death sequences and can draft appropriate language —
Wills available on the web probably not-so-much. Here's the age-
old existentialist debate: *per stirpes or per capita?*

* *Who should administer the estate?*

When a Will is probated (bills paid and gifts distributed), the
person in charge is known as the *personal representative* (in older
language, still favored in some states, on late-night movies and in
popular imagination, the term might be *executor, executrix, ad-
ministrator or administratrix*). Choosing a personal representative
is important. Family trust, competence and honesty are critical,
especially in the case of remarriage, where blended families will
be involved and fights over probate can be bitter. Consider joint
executors—one Hatfield, one McCoy.

* *Homes and Businesses*

If a family home or business is involved, consult a lawyer. Bad
mistakes can be made.

* *Cutting someone out*

The only one you *can't* cut out (in most states) is one's current spouse who will take one-third or one-half of the property, or
perhaps half of what was acquired during marriage. One can usually cut out a spouse *only* if the spouse signed a prenuptial or post-
nuptial agreement, giving up all claims, or in the case of abandonment or legal separation. If you want to cut one of your children out, it is good practice to *mention* them by name so they can
not later claim you just forgot about them.

* *Will the Will cause family friction?*

Sometimes children will not be treated equally. One might
have special needs or maybe has already received money or prop-

erty. To avoid bitterness (there is nothing worse for a child than to think their parent loved a sibling more), it is best to explain these choices to the family.

*Holographic Wills*

You may have heard of these, the first choice of nervous flyers everywhere.

*If I die before I land,*

*This is my stuff, I do hand . . .*

Most states do *not* recognize them. Those that do have differing requirements but all require that the material parts be *entirely* in the testator's handwriting (no Word Perfect). As a stop gap measure before writing a formal one, they can't hurt. There's no set form:

*Holographic Wills don't have to rhyme,*

*After writing, just date and sign.*

# CHAPTER 25

# Avoiding Probate, Gifts, Life Insurance, Joint Ownership, IRAs

*In the movie Ghostbusters, Bill Murray removes ghosts from haunted houses. This brings him into close contact with them. He has one rule—"Never have romantic relations with a ghost." This works well enough until he meets a very seductive ghost. "Well, it really isn't a rule," he muses, "it's more of a guideline."*

### Avoiding Probate

Despite the hype of self-help books, which have turned "probate" into "plague," avoiding it isn't even a good guideline. The devices we describe will help avoid probate, but they shouldn't be chosen for that; they should be chosen only if they make sense.

Probate is simply a *court process* of gathering the assets that remain in a decedent's estate, paying the bills, and distributing what's left according to the Will, and if there isn't one, according to the state's intestacy laws. *One good thing about probate:* distribution will be supervised by the court and, if there are disputes about who gets what, they will be resolved by a judge. So how did probate get its bad name?

Historically it was expensive and lengthy. Until the court formally approves changes in title, the family cannot sell or borrow on the property, stocks, or saving accounts, and the delay can cause family hardships. However most states provide for "family allowances" during the probate process, which allow for immediate *distributions. Joint checking* or *saving accounts* with the right of survivorship also can solve the cash-flow problem.

Many (but not all) states now have informal, inexpensive, and fairly quick probate processes. With smaller estates, surviving heirs simply file a document with the court and the clerk will walk them through the steps. No lawyers! *In these states, the costs and hassles of avoiding probate can be worse than probate itself.* In some states, however, probate remains a problem, New York, California, and Illinois, to name a few.

To avoid probate, simply get one's property out of one's estate; put it in a Trust or IRA, give it away, use it to buy life insurance, or put it in joint tenancy. We will look at Trusts in the next chapters.

Two essential points.

\* Folks still need a Will. It is a fool's errand to die nearly broke; Wills can deal with what remains and, as we have seen in the last chapter, can accomplish other goals.

\* Don't confuse *avoiding probate* with *avoiding estate taxes.* Much of the money moved out of the estate as a method of *avoiding probate* will still be counted as part of your estate for tax purposes. However estate taxes are not a concern for most (you gotta be rich).

*Lifetime Gifts*

Giving is one of life's joys and, better still, there are few tax consequences. Recipients of gifts pay *no* taxes on them. Gifts to recognized charities are tax deductible under federal and many state laws. Large gifts to individuals, at the writing *over* $13,000 per year (or $26,000 for married couples) must be *reported* by filing a gift return; the excess will be counted as part of one's estate at time of death for estate tax purposes.

Be aware of the tax problem in the case of *appreciated assets,* such as property and stocks. Passed at death, the beneficiary gets a *stepped-up basis*; if by lifetime gift, the beneficiary takes the owner's original basis.

> *A stock purchased for $100,000 is now worth $250,000. Given as a lifetime gift the recipient has a $100,000 basis, meaning if it is sold there will be a taxable capital gain of $150,000. On the other hand, if passed under a Will, the recipient will have a stepped-up basis, the worth of the asset at the time of death, here $250,000. There will be no capital gain if sold for that amount.*

*Gifts to Minors and Mentally Disabled Recipients*

Minors do not have contractual capacity and will not be able to sell the property, even to pay for emergencies. Most likely, the parents will not be able to sell the gifted property either. A guardian or conservator will have to be appointed for the child. We have had just this happen several times: a mother, thinking she is protecting the family home from creditors puts the home in her children's name. When she decides to move a court proceeding is required to sell the home *and* the proceeds go into a conservatorship for the children. To make matters even worse, when each child turns 18, he or she is outright owner of the proceeds and may buy nose rings.

*The Uniform Transfers to Minors Act* allows the donor of a gift to name a parent or other responsible adult to be the custodian. The income on the gift will be taxed at the parent's rate until the child is 14 and the gift will be considered available to the child, which may mean less college financial aid. In most states the child will be entitled to get the money outright at age 21.

Special Trusts are now available for educational expenses. The most popular are known as "Section 529 plans" after the section of the Internal Revenue Code providing favorable tax treatment. Check with your bank or broker.

Use Trusts for *major* gifts to support grandchildren's education. We'll tell you how in the next chapter.

*Mentally disabled adults* do not have contractual capacity and may squander money. Again, Trusts are a solution. If the person is receiving public assistance, the money may make the person ineligible. Carefully drafted Trusts (usually called *"Special Needs Trusts"*) can avoid this problem.

*Life insurance*

Beneficiaries collect by simply presenting the death certificate to the insurance company making life insurance an attractive estate planning tool. Probate, even in the best of cases, takes time—and proceeds from life insurance policies may come in handy. The proceeds from life insurance do not pass through the estate and are usually not subject to its creditors.

On the other hand, some advise folks to cancel life insurance policies because their kids are grown and to buy long term care policies instead. As we age, the need for insurance may shift—from providing for our families at death to providing for ourselves at incapacity.

*Joint Ownership*

Some tout joint ownership of property and stocks as the best way of avoiding probate. However except for *smaller* items, such as a car and relatively small bank accounts, *joint ownership is usually not a good idea.*

* There are several forms of joint ownership; only some have a "right of survivorship" which vests title in one joint owner at the time the other dies. *Without* such a survivorship aspect, joint ownership does not avoid probate: at the death of one joint owner, his or her share stays in his or her estate.

* Joint ownership presents problems if both owners die at the same time, and may have adverse income, gift, and estate tax consequences.

* Joint ownership means giving up unfettered control over the asset.

*Many married couples hold title to their house as joint tenants with right of survivorship, and usually (but not always) this works out just fine. But assume a couple has been separated for several years, with the wife living in the house. In her Will she leaves everything to her daughter. When she dies, however, the daughter will not get the mother's interest in the house: it passes, without probate, to the surviving husband who is now free to sell it or leave it to anyone he wishes.*

* As long as property is in joint ownership, the creditors of the other person can reach it.

\* In some states, joint ownership won't even speed transfer of assets upon death, and some states automatically freeze joint accounts until tax officials can check things out. (Bank employees read the obits.)

\*Joint tenancy assets are still included in your estate for purposes of calculating your estate tax, at least to the extent that you were the one who put the money into the asset.

*Annuities, IRAs, and Roth IRA*

IRAs and Roth IRAs are good ways to pass money; ownership passes to the designed beneficiaries *without* going through probate and being vulnerable to estate creditors

Advise folks to *check to see who they listed as beneficiaries . . . times change.* In our experience, clients are often wrong when they try and remember how they filled out beneficiary designations.

With a traditional IRA (or a 401(k) and similar retirement plans) one must start withdrawing money in the year after the year in which one turns 70 ½. (Don't ask). In the first years this will require withdrawal of about 4% of the total amount, going to about 8% at the age of 88. Account owners will pay income taxes on the amounts they withdraw.

A *Roth IRA* requires *no withdrawals* by the owner, thus leaving more for designated heirs. And whatever money is withdrawn (after the first five years have passed) is tax *free*. That is because contributions to Roth IRAs are not deductible when they are made, and they earn money over the years as tax-free income.

One can convert an IRA or other retirement account into a Roth IRA but income taxes must be paid at the time.

When an IRA, 401(k), Roth IRA or other retirement account owner dies, the rules get complicated—unless the owner's surviving spouse is named as beneficiary.

## Beneficiary Designations—Poor Man's Trusts

*POD (payable on death)*, *TOD (transfer on death)*, or *ITF (in-trust)* accounts transfer funds (or perhaps property) on death of the owner—but not to convey any *present* interest in the beneficiary. These avoid probate without requiring a Trust (with some cost savings, as an attorney may not be involved). Clients often fail to appreciate the importance of monitoring and updating their beneficiary designations as children mature, marry, have children of their own, divorce, become spendthrifts or otherwise unreliable, and even die before their parents.

## Living Trusts

Assets in a *Living Trust* avoid probate and one advantage it has over the other estate planning devices (such as Wills and various forms of joint ownership), is that it a solves the problem of having someone else manage one's financial affairs in the event of disability. That is, a Living Trust has many of the advantages of a Durable Power of Attorney. But before we turn to Living Trusts we will describe the most wonderful legal device of all—the Trust!

# CHAPTER 26

# Trusts: Legal Shmoos

*In the comic strip Li'l Abner the Shmoos were unique beings that did just about everything—shopped, cleaned, set the table—and then cooked themselves for dinner.*

Trusts are like that. They do about everything. The *trustor*, *grantor* or *settlor*, gives money or property to a *trustee* (a bank, a friend, or, as we will see, *themselves*) to be managed and used in trust for the benefit of the *beneficiary* (a minor child, a disabled relative, or, as we will see, *themselves*). The money or property is to be used as directed by the *trust instrument* ("for the college education of my grandchildren" or "for the medical care of my niece Joanna").

*Advantages of Trusts*

*\* Privacy*

Trusts can act like Wills in that they can be used to distribute property but they are more private. Wills are administered under court supervision and assets and beneficiaries are public; but not so with Trusts which are administered by the trustee. This can be good or bad news depending on the honesty and competence of the trustee.

## * Timing of Gifts

Unlike Wills, Trusts allow one to delay and structure gifts, money for grandchildren's education or for lifetime support for a disabled nephew. Trusts can be tailored:

> *"The trustee shall accumulate interest until my grandchild enrolls in college and then the trustee will pay for tuition, room and board, and necessary books for four years of college and any graduate education thereafter. After my grandchild finishes his education, the trustee shall pay him the interest on the Trust until he turns 40 years old, and then the principal shall be distributed, one-half to him and one-half to the Denial of Death Foundation."*

Trusts can be created during one's life (called *Inter Vivos Trusts*) or as part of one's Will (*Testamentary Trusts*). A *stand by Trust* is created during life, funded nominally, and then funded at death under one's Will.

## * The Rule Against Perpetuities

> *My beloved country estate, Blackacre, I leave in trust for my first-born son, for his use during his lifetime, and thereafter for the use of his first-born son and thereafter for the use of his first-born son, etc., etc., etc.*

English judges, who gave us much of our common law, were not fools. If these Trusts stood up, neither they (nor *their* first-born sons) were likely to get very much of anything. (It was, by the way, *always* the first-born *son*.) So these judges came up with the *Rule Against Perpetuities*. It is so complicated that no one really understands it but it basically means at some point you will have to let your incompetent heirs finally get their grubby hands on your property. Trusts can last only for *a life in being plus 21 years,* which is much easier to say than figure out. In recent years, various states have lengthened the Rule Against Perpetuities to various terms (commonly 500 years or so) or have eliminated the Rule altogether.

*Issues to Consider*

*\* Trusts for the Disabled*

Income paid to the beneficiary may make the individual ineligible for welfare assistance. A *Special Needs Trust* solves this problem: the beneficiary can receive some benefits (for travel, entertainment, education, extra therapy, furniture, paid companionship, or almost anything but cash, food or shelter) without any effect on welfare services. In some cases it might even be both possible and advisable for the Special Needs Trust to provide food and shelter.

*\* Revocable or Irrevocable?*

Revocable Trusts allow the trustors to change their mind and get their property back. However, their creditors can reach it and earned income goes on their individual returns.

The most common use of Irrevocable Trusts is to fund life insurance policies on the trustor's life. This gets the life insurance out of the insured's estate for tax purposes, without giving the policy outright to the kids (maybe they can't be relied on to keep the insurance current). The second most common Irrevocable Trust: the Special Needs Trust.

*Administration: Conflict between current and later beneficiaries*

English novels teach us that trustees tend to be conservative (at least when they're not falling in love with their shy, beautiful ward, who is, in turn, madly in love with a poor but struggling—yet destined for greatness—doctor). But it's actually hard to be a trustee, even without the complications of romance (or romance novels).

Trustees are in a bind. They have obligations both to the *current* beneficiary and to the *remainder* beneficiaries (those folks who take what's left in the Trust when it ends). If the trustee is too free and easy giving the current beneficiary money, or invests the Trust's assets only for the benefit of the income recipient, he may be sued by the remainder beneficiaries. Help out.

*I intend that the provisions of this Trust be liberally construed and that the term "education" include trade and art schools, educational travel and all necessary expenses related thereto, including the purchase, maintenance, operation and insuring of a car.*

*       *       *

*In making discretionary distributions and investments, the trustee is to consider first the interests of the income beneficiary; the trustee has express authority to distribute trust principal even to the exhaustion of the trust estate if she, in her sole discretion, deems it appropriate to do so.*

*Powers of the Trustee*

What the trustee can and can't do will be a matter of state law. Still, consider:

\* No power to buy speculative stocks, or options? No power to buy "sin" stocks or invest in off shore accounts.

\* Authority to invade principal to handle emergencies.

\* Power to make gifts, settle claims and hire accountants.

*\* Choosing the Trustee*

Banks will not get involved unless the Trust is large, in the range of $150,000 to $500,000. For smaller Trusts, relatives are often used. Should they receive a fee? Consider the trustee's relation to the beneficiaries, financial skills, age in relation to beneficiaries and geographical proximity. Always name an alternative or successor trustee, just in case. Co-trustees are possible, perhaps a bank for wisdom and a relative for compassion.

*A dying woman named her beloved manicurist as the trustee. Unfortunately, the manicurist didn't know finances and lost the entire million dollars.*

You can read this story broadly ("competence" trumps "beloved") or narrowly (don't appoint your manicurist).

# CHAPTER 27

# Living Trusts

In the comedy Raising Arizona, a baby is kidnapped and one mean-looking bounty-hunter approaches the father offering to find the baby for him.

"Why should I hire you?" the father asks. "The police are on it."

"If ya want to find your baby, ask me. If ya want to find a donut, ask the police."

Can we make it fit?

"If you want a free donut, go to a Living Trust Seminar. If you want a Living Trust, go to a lawyer. "

Today's hot item is the Living Trust, sold at free breakfasts. The price ranges from $900 to $1,500. The pitch?

* You will avoid probate and won't need a Will!

* If you (God forbid!) become incapable of managing your finances, you won't need a Guardianship!

127

Nine out of ten people who purchase Living Trusts *don't need them*. There are cheaper and easier ways of accomplishing the same things.

But first, what is a "Living" Trust, and how does it differ from a (no modifier) "Trust" as described in the previous Chapter? It usually refers to a self-declared Trust, established while living and naming the Trust's creator(s) as trustee(s). But not always. That simple structure, though, is what we are talking about here: a Trust created by one individual or a couple, naming himself, herself or themselves as trustee, and providing for his/her/their benefit during life and distribution to named heirs at death. Let's look at one.

### The Living Trust of Billy and Sandy Knowles

*The assets of this Trust shall be used for the benefit of Billy and Sandy Knowles, husband and wife, and shall be administered by them. In the event that they become incapable of administering this Trust, it shall be administered by their son, Matthew, or, if he cannot, by the First National Bank. At the death of either Billy or Sandy, this Trust shall become irrevocable. Thereafter, the assets of the Trust will be used for the benefit of the survivor. At the death of the survivor, the assets remaining in the Trust shall be distributed in equal parts to the then surviving children of Billy and Sandy.*

Let's review the language.

*"for the benefit of Billy and Sandy Knowles, husband and wife, and shall be administered by them."*

Not much has changed. Billy and Sandy continue to manage their financial affairs as before, but now must sign as "trustees."

*"At the death of either, this Trust shall become irrevocable."*

Until the death of either, the Trust is *revocable*. They can change their minds and take everything out of the Trust. Income it earns will go on their individual return. Once a Trust becomes irrevocable, then it becomes a separate tax entity, will have to get its own tax number, and will have to pay its own taxes.

Most importantly, when the Trust becomes irrevocable, the surviving spouse *cannot* change who gets the remainder when the Trust ends. This solves the problem of the "blended family" which we discuss when we discuss remarriage.

*"In the event that Billy and Sandy become incapable of administering this Trust, it shall be administered by their son, Matthew or, if he cannot, by the First National Bank."*

Here the Living Trust is acting like a Durable Power of Attorney. Note that there is a potential conflict of interest in having Matthew act as guardian. As he will share in what is left in the Trust, he may be tempted to skimp. Maybe you can tighten this up with instructions as to how the money should be used, *"If either Billy or Sandy need nursing home care, the trustee should spend whatever is necessary to make them comfortable, including private rooms and nursing."*

*"At the death of the survivor, the assets remaining in the Trust shall be distributed in equal parts to the then surviving children of Billy and Sandy."*

Here the Living Trust is acting like a Will. Fair enough, but don't skim. The assets go to the "then surviving children." Pause and consider the implications of that. What if they have a son and a daughter, the daughter has two children and dies before her parents? As written the grandkids get nothing (though state law may imply an intent to benefit descendants). Or what if the surviving children are 9 and 12 years old? Should they get the money outright? And what happens when Billy dies and Sandy wants to make changes?

In the simplest of language lurk legal problems. The hardest thing of all is seeing what's not there:

*"Being of sound mind . . ."*

This is known as the sanity clause; in *Duck Soup* Harpo dismissed it "I don't believe in no sanity clause." Living Trusts don't believe in them either. No pomposity for them. It's coffee and donuts time. Impress on your clients that what they sign will affect their life, their spouse's and their family's. Ponderous language reminds us of that. Yet another of life's hard choices: family's well-being or a donut.

# Health Care Documents

*Everyone* should have a *Living Will* and a *Health Care Power of Attorney*. These documents *must* be stored in a safe place where others can find them.

Documents can take you only so far. Even the best-drafted will be somewhat ambiguous and family disputes may arise. *Family conversations* are key in assuring one's wishes will be carried out. We discuss them in *Confronting the Elephant*.

### Living Wills

Probably everyone has one, even though they don't know where it is or what it says. Living Wills state what kind of medical treatment one wants, or doesn't want if dying and no longer mentally competent. On the web there are Living Will forms that cover, in depressing detail, every horrible disease and intrusive treatment that flesh is heir to. Most are of the variety of "If I am in a vegetative state, no heroic measures." Studies show, however, that even the best drafted Living Wills are often ignored; doctors do what the family wants. This makes sense: one's family will know a lot more about the current situation than the patient did sitting in a lawyer's office checking boxes. Still a Living Will can't hurt.

You might prefer "I want everything possible done to keep me alive, hang the expense."

*Health Care Power of Attorney*

This appoints an agent to make medical decisions *anytime* the person is unable to do so, due to unconsciousness or mental incompetence. Living Wills are effective only if the person is in a terminal state. Three questions:

*Who should be the agent?* Not one's spouse. He or she may be sick, depressed or confused. Usually children or long-time friends are better choices. If one child is selected but not another, wisdom would dictate explaining. Appoint a back-up.

*What powers do you want the agent to have?* Unless the document authorizes it, the agent may not have the power to move individuals to a *nursing home* or to take them from the hospital against doctors' advice. And, unless the document says otherwise, the agent may not have the power to remove life supports. (It is often best never to agree to have them installed.) That's where the Living Will comes in.

*Where to get the documents?* The Web has forms but it wiser to veer on the safe side and have a lawyer draft these documents as they can write them to reflect the individual's specific wishes. Besides, the more bells and whistles, the more likely doctors and hospitals will pay attention. Lawyers usually prepare these documents as part of an estate plan (and keep copies in their files). In some states (and in some hospitals), however, it might make sense to rely on the state-approved form. State law might require it.

*What if these documents aren't executed (or found)?*

Many states have *Surrogacy Statutes* or *Family Agency Acts* listing folks who can make medical decisions when the patient can't. Where they exist, they usually list a spouse first, then children, then other relatives and, in a few states, domestic partners. They might even include medical providers, with some protections to assure disinterested oversight.

No discussion of documents would be complete without:

*Do Not Resuscitate (DNR)*

*Code Blue* with its zapping and chest pounding works about 90% of the time on *ER* and *House*. In real life less than 20% survive the event and, of the survivors, over 80% of them are dead within a year. A DNR (Do Not Resuscitate) order (usually available in the hospital) directs health care workers to back off and let nature do its work.

Folks who do not want to be "rescued" by paramedics at home or elsewhere can fill out specialized directives. Often they are posted on the frig or put in the freezer. State laws and procedures vary widely on DNR designations and advance directives prohibiting resuscitation; check. You might ask about your community's involvement in the POLST (Physicians Orders on Life-Sustaining Treatment) movement.

Without directives to the contrary, EMTs will always try to save lives, no matter the pain, no matter the odds. One remarked, "That's what we are trained to do. If it is clear a loved one doesn't want interventions, just don't call us immediately."

*PART 8*

# Dying – The Details

*CHAPTER 29*

# Death in the Family

*The First Few Days: Funeral Homes and Burial*

Funeral homes can be called at any hour. They will take care of official notifications and will arrange for copies of the official death certificate needed in notifying insurance companies, Social Security, and retirement plans. Obituaries in local papers can be arranged by the funeral home at a modest cost.

The average cost of a funeral, incidentally, is about $6,500, according to the National Funeral Directors Association. That does not include the cost of a burial plot or other cemetery expenses. Before you put down a credit card or write a check, take a look at the decedent's Will and see whether he prepaid for his funeral, or left specific wishes as to where he wanted to be scattered or buried.

There are strong psychological pressures to overspend, not wanting to appear "cheap." Bad idea to agree to a price on the first visit; good idea to go home and think how else the money can be spent.

Cremation is less expensive. Ashes can be scattered where permitted and permanent urns are available, some are quite beautiful and moving, others fanciful, such as the ones adorned with statuettes of golfers. Cremation is also more accepted and widespread than ever before. About a quarter of U.S. deaths led to cremation as recently as 2000; the number now is more than one in three and headed to more than half of all deaths by about 2020. As we write Mississippi and Alabama have cremation rates below 15%, and Nevada and Hawaii nearly 70%. Interesting.

Under rule of the Federal Trade Commission funeral directors must disclose the cost of all goods and services, even over the phone, and provide written lists. Funeral products can be purchased separately; no need not buy entire packages. Funeral directors familiar with the prior rules (the current ones were adopted in 1982) report to us that the average spent by families actually went *up* at first—turned out customers just wanted straight information and detailed price lists. Imagine that.

*Autopsies.* Post-death surgeries designed to determine the cause of death might disclose genetic diseases unknown to the family so that steps can be taken to avoid them. Conversely, they might discover that Granddad wasn't suffering from the genetic disease his family feared. The law requires an autopsy if the cause of death is suspicious or unknown, and depending on state law if the individual died within a year of surgery or died without a physician present to certify the cause of death.

*Organ Donation.* Even if the decedent (by Will, donation card, or driver-license designation) indicated a desire to donate, often hospitals will seek the family's agreement. If the decedent left no instructions, usually the family can authorize the donation. Some families have religious and similar objections to donations. However, some object in the mistaken belief that they would delay the funeral, prevent a viewing, or increase the funeral cost. Generally they don't.

### The First Few Weeks: Cash, Bills, and Notifications

#### Cash

If there is money in joint saving and checking accounts, no problem. Same is true if the money is in a Living Trust. Some advise keeping large amounts of cash in joint safety deposit boxes, the idea being that upon the death of one, the other can easily get to the cash and that the cash will not show up as part of the estate, thus cutting taxes. This isn't good advice. First, as to easy access, joint checking and savings accounts achieve the same goal. Second, as to avoiding taxes, it's against the law. And banks read the obituaries. In some states they may seal joint safety deposit boxes, which can only then be opened in the presence of a state official (this is now much less common).

If the family's assets were kept in the decedent's name alone, there may be trouble. Immediately open a Probate Proceeding. Most states provide for a *family allowance* to support spouses and dependent minor children during probate.

#### Bills

Let things sort themselves out before paying the decedent's bills, such as medical and nursing home bills. If the estate is to be probated, the estate will pay the bills; if there is a Living Trust, the trustee will. As a general rule, only the person (or his or her estate) who received the service is liable to pay the bill. Generally, family members (children and spouses) are not required to pay the bills out of their own pockets. This may be different in the community property states (Arizona, California, Idaho, Louisiana, Nevada, New Mexico, Texas, Washington and Wisconsin).

Some of the bills sent to a decedent after his death may even be bogus. Scam artists take advantage of a family's distress. If creditors are getting pushy, send them a letter explaining that the individual has died and that you will need time to sort out his affairs.

On the other hand, continue to pay ongoing bills, such as rent, utilities, and, yes, the lawyer's fees for probate. If these bills are not paid, the services will stop.

*Notifications and titles*

If cars and property were co-owned by the decedent, the governmental agency in charge of the titles should be contacted to reissue the title in the survivor's name.

Life insurance companies should be notified. If the decedent was working at the time, the employer should be asked if the company maintained life insurance on its employees.

If the decedent was covered by Social Security (most jobs), call Social Security for current information on possible benefits. Folks who might be entitled to benefits include *dependent children, dependent parents, surviving spouses,* and even if the couple was not married, the survivor if they had, or adopted, a child together.

There is a small Social Security death benefit for surviving spouses in limited circumstances. It is not a lot of money; it has been stuck at $255 for decades, and it is generally only payable to a surviving spouse.

*CHAPTER 30*

# Probate and Disgruntled Heirs

This chapter is boring. We'll spice it up with allegations of murder.

Probate is a court proceeding to wind up a decedent's estate, pay the bills and distribute what's left according to the decedent's Will or, if there isn't one, under the state's intestacy law. In most cases big time probate isn't necessary (except to scare people into buying one's book). How come?

*Personal property*, stuff that doesn't have a "title" (furniture, heirlooms, jewelry, computers, pets) can simply be distributed in the family, unless there is a Will that directs its distribution. It is far better if "who gets what" is worked out before the decedent dies—fights over who gets the Grandfather Clock destroy families.

*Property with titles.* Cars, houses, land, stock, bonds, have "title" and before the family can sell them, the title must be rewritten. Usually that's not much of a problem. If the title shows a co-owner, indicating the right of survivorship, the co-owner simply shows the death certificate to the appropriate official (in some circumstances and states the death certificate may not even be required). With cars, the appropriate official is the DMV, with land and houses the County Recorder or Clerk. For stocks, bonds, brokerage and bank accounts, simply present a death certificate at the appropriate office.

If the title is *only* in the name of the decedent probate may be needed. However, if not much property is involved, most states allow for quick and inexpensive probate, usually involving simply filling out a form and attaching a death certificate. Big time probate is usually reserved for the rich.

*The Probate Process*

Any interested party, usually the spouse or an adult child, can petition the Probate Court to take jurisdiction over a decedent's estate. In smaller estates, a relative can do this simply by going to the courthouse and filling out the correct papers. In larger estates, a lawyer should be retained. In any event, this should be done quickly, as someone must be authorized to take possession of the individual's assets.

Once the Will has been established, the court will appoint a person to take charge, often called a "personal representative." The first job is to find and protect the decedent's assets, going through bank accounts, deposit boxes, talking to stock brokers, and going through the personal papers (learning that mild Aunt Jane was really a CIA agent). Then creditors must be notified—in person or by ads in the paper. It's "snooze you lose" for them.

After the bills are paid, what's left goes to the heirs. If there is a Will, well, then, you need to know just a little more. There are three kinds of bequests:

Specific bequests (objects): To my only daughter, my 1956 Studebaker.

*General (or "pecuniary") bequests* (money): To my only son, $75,000.

*Residuary bequest* (remainder): To my then living grandchildren, divided equally, the remainder of my estate.

Well and good. But what happens if there is not enough in the estate to make good on all the bequests? Say the Studebaker was sold prior to Dad's death, or that Dad gave it to the Studebaker Hawks Club? Does the daughter get nothing? What if there is a Studebaker but no $75,000? Does the son get nothing? This gets complicated and you'll need legal advice. Even if you end up getting nothing, worse things can happen. Read *Bleak House*.

### Disgruntled Heirs

Will contests are rare but to ignore disgruntled heirs is risky! They are folks who would get more under the law of intestacy than they get under the Will (or Trust), or someone who would have gotten more under the Will but the lawyer who drafted the Will messed up.

Say that Daddy Warbucks wanted to leave Little Annie money to remove the dots in her eyes but she never got it because the lawyer drafting his Will did so negligently. (Maybe this chapter isn't as boring as we feared.) In some states Annie can sue the lawyer as a "third party beneficiary" of the contract between Warbucks and his lawyer.

Disgruntled heirs include:

*Surviving spouses.* Unless there is a prenuptial agreement, and no matter what the Will says, surviving spouses are entitled to something: often a third of the estate (half, in some jurisdictions— or a flat dollar amount, in others).

*Forgotten children.* Natural, adopted and illegitimate children not named in the Will can argue that the decedent didn't mean to cut them out, only forgot them. "As to my son Samson, who insisted on never cutting his hair, I give nothing" at least makes clear Manoah (Samson's father) remembered he had a son.

*Children born, and spouses married, after the Will was written.* The claim is that the decedent didn't mean to cut them out. State law may take care of that claim, providing in many cases that such "pretermitted" heirs take a share equal to that they would have received if no Will had been written.

*Children of prior marriages.* Some couples upon remarriage agree to leave everything to the survivor promising that when the survivor dies the estate will be split between their respective children. Tempted by dark forces, the surviving spouse may renege and leave everything to his or her own children. We saw earlier that a Living Trust can address this problem. Disappointed children may have a claim but it will be an uphill fight.

*Heirs who suspect lack of capacity.* The stock opening is *"Being of sound mind"* (We prefer *"It was the best of times, planning for the worst of times."*) If the testator lost legal capacity before signing the Will (or Trust), it is invalid and the estate passes under the intestacy law.

*Heirs who suspect undue influence.* Large gifts to nurses, neighbors, and TV evangelists are suspect. Was the person in a position to assert control over the testator by threats or by withholding care?

*Heirs who suspect murder.* A murderer cannot inherit from the victim, even if named in the Will ("Someday, son, all of this will be yours."). There is a legal maxim—"You cannot profit from your own wrong." Given the nature of the world, however, this maxim is more inspirational than descriptive.

However, if Sis can prove Bro did in dear old Dad, he can't get a nickel and there's more for Sis. Someone most always profits from wrong.

If one suspects both undue influence and murder, throw in a few good trial scenes and a little sex, and you got yourself a novel. But probably not *Bleak House*.

# CHAPTER 31

# Ending Life: Pulling Plugs, Euthanasia, and Suicide

*Ending Medical Treatment*

> *A patient, age 80, lies unconscious, hooked to feeding and hydration tubes. There has been no improvement for days. Medicated with morphine, there are no signs of pain. Physicians say that in all likelihood the patient will never regain consciousness and will have permanent and extensive brain damage. The doctors ask the patient's adult child what to do.*

An agonizing decision. Living Wills and Durable Health Care Powers of Attorney help. So too family conversations about end-of-life matters.

In 1990, the United States Supreme Court backhandedly confirmed the right of a competent patient to order the removal of life-sustaining systems. It also discussed some of the rules concerning the *incompetent* patient. A guardian can order the removal of life-sustaining treatment but, before this can be done, a state can insist that the guardian *prove* that the patient, before becoming incompetent, expressed a desire that this be done. The state can require that this showing be made by *clear and convincing evidence*. But your state probably does not have such a high requirement—unless you live in Missouri, Massachusetts or New York. <u>Your state probably allows guardians to make the decision based on the notion of "substituted judgment"</u>—the idea that a guardian should <u>try to do what his or her ward would do if competent.</u> If there is a family fight over what to do, or if doctors refuse to terminate treatment, a court hearing may be necessary. State law varies and is changing.

*state require proof of patients desires*

### Feeding and Hydration Tubes

In the absence of artificially-supplied food and fluids, a patient will usually die of dehydration, not starving, within (in most cases) about ten days to two weeks. Efforts will be made to relieve dry mouth and thirst. Is this a particularly painful way to go? A study in 1994 indicated that only 13% of those who died this way experienced discomfort. Still, some did and there may be more recent studies. Of course, the pain of this kind of death must be balanced against the pain the patient is currently experiencing.

*It is far easier to keep feeding and hydration tubes out than it is to get them out.* This is true as a practical matter, even though most state laws and ethical precepts agree that there is no difference between the decision to withhold and the decision to withdraw. If a loved one is in a nursing home and the staff recommends such tubes, think long and hard before authorizing them. They have a financial interest in keeping the patient alive, no matter how dismal the prospects and no matter how painful the condition. Once the tubes are in, it may take a court order—or at least an extraordinary amount of effort and angst—to get them out.

*Euthanasia and Death with Dignity Laws*

> *In 1998 an Oregon woman, dying of breast cancer, became the first person to use Oregon's Death with Dignity Law. She died peacefully in her sleep, at home, surrounded by her family. Her physician had given her medication; five minutes later she was asleep, thirty minutes later, dead.*

Euthanasia involves taking *active* steps to *cause* death. It is *not* the same as removing life-sustaining help. The distinction between action and inaction is as old as our common law. Shakespeare skewered it. In *Hamlet*, Ophelia is to be given a Christian burial, one denied to suicides. "How can this be, unless she drowned herself in her own defense?" asked one character. The grave digger explained:

> *"Here lies the water; good: here stands the man; good: if the man go to the water, and drown himself, it is, will he, nill he, he goes—mark you that; but if the water come to him and drown him, he drowns not himself."*

Helping another to commit suicide is criminal. It is not a defense that the victim wanted to die, asked for the help, was in great pain, or would have died anyway—or that the act was motivated by love and compassion. The primary exceptions to the ban on assisting suicide, and it is a narrow one, is the Death with Dignity Laws which allow doctors to prescribe, but not to administer, drugs that kill. The patient must self-administer the lethal drugs.

Under the laws in Oregon and Washington, two physicians must certify that the patient (1) has, to a reasonable medical certainty, no more than six months to live, (2) is competent, (3) has been informed of alternatives to suicide (hospice, pain control), and (4) is making a voluntary choice in requesting the lethal prescription. If the patient is depressed or suffering mental illness, no prescription will be written. Nor will one be written until at least fifteen days after the initial request, and only then if the patient repeats the request. If all of these steps are properly taken, the physicians will not be civilly or criminally liable for writing the prescription and, if the patient takes the medications, it will not be deemed a suicide for life insurance purposes.

There has been no rush. In Oregon it accounts for 1 in 500 deaths, (around 600) and in Washington, 1 in 1,000. Patients who used the law are about equally divided by sex, overwhelmingly white, well-educated and financially comfortable. They made the choice not to avoid pain, but rather out of a desire to control their lives. Most had cancer or Lou Gehrig's disease.

Is assisted suicide a good idea?

There are very strong and convincing arguments on both sides. In support, there is the notion that freedom and, indeed, being human entails the right to captain one's own destiny. Why shouldn't you have the right to end your own life, and to seek medical help to do so? Why shouldn't you be allowed to avoid the great pain and expense generally associated with final illness?

Another less obvious argument in favor of physician-assisted suicide: it may actually *reduce* suicide. Many elderly, suffering from chronic illness, fear that it will eventually lead to unbearable suffering and that, when it does come, they will no longer have the ability to end it themselves. In panic, they take their own lives. The mere promise that, if that time arrives, there will be someone there for them could stay their hand and immediately relieve their consuming fear. Most people who have "saved up pills, just in case," never use them.

But there are strong philosophical and religious concerns against condoning any form of suicide. No one should play God; the guiding principle of medicine is "first, do no harm," and legalized suicide, even if not widespread, will lead to a general cheapening of human life. There are practical concerns as well: if assisted suicide is available, how can relatives be prevented from dumping expensive or inconvenient relatives? From trying to accelerate their inheritance?

There is concern of the slippery slope. Although most proposals to legalize assisted suicide, like the one in Oregon, are restricted to consenting adults who have a terminal illness, the fear is that these limits cannot hold. Why deny a consenting adult medical help in ending a life made unbearable by severe chronic fatal illness, such as Lou Gehrig's Disease, simply because that disease has not yet progressed to the "terminal stage". Condoning suicide may slowly but surely lead to involuntary euthanasia. To acknowledge that some lives aren't worth living, the next step may be to put severely retarded or disabled individuals "out of their misery." Fanciful? One hears arguments that the elderly have a "duty" to step aside, and a group of severely disabled individuals, fiercely opposed to physician-assisted suicide, calls itself "Not Dead Yet." We, as a society, have too much history with eugenics and social engineering to be trusted with this tool, or so the argument goes.

*Double effect pain medication*

Pain relief, which has the *unintended* result of causing death, is neither suicide nor euthanasia. Physicians prescribe morphine for certain painful cancers; as the pain increases, so, too, the dosages. Increased dosages increase suppression of breathing and heart rate, and may eventually lead to death. This is known as a treatment's "double effect."

## Suicide

There are how-to books and there are advocates. But consider:

*Depression can be treated and is often transitory. "This too shall pass."

*Almost all pain can be alleviated by proper medication. The reason that many die painful deaths is not the inability of medicine to control pain, but the lack of training of most doctors in dealing with terminal illness and their reluctance to prescribe high enough dosages. Hospice, and the relatively modern pain management movement, promise adequate painkiller dosages and hence a relatively pain-free death.

* Suicide of a loved one is one of the hardest deaths to get over—guilt abounds ("Was this my fault?"). The message you send to relatives and family is of darkest human despair: "Some lives aren't worth living."

Finally, let's talk brass tacks. If your choice is to jump or to crash your car, you may go out as a murderer. If you choose a gun, it's messy. Who will find your bloody body? Who will be cursed forever by the image?

If you are feeling suicidal, talk to family, friends and spiritual advisers. If you don't, you do them a double wrong: your death and your cruel denial of their opportunity to reach out to comfort you.

# Hospice

---

*"Why did we wait so long? We should have done it months earlier. It would have been so much better for him, so much better for us. We could have spent the time together, not in hospital waiting rooms."*

*Hospice is not just for cancer patients.*

Anyone likely die within the next *six months* can receive hospice care.

*It's not a place, hospice can come to your home.*

There are hospices in hospitals and other locations but services can be provided at home. Hospice will provide the needed equipment such as beds.

*It's not just nurses, it's a team.*

The team is composed of nurses, doctors, counselors and trained volunteers. They love their jobs and find deep satisfaction helping others.

*It's not just for the patient, it's for the family.*

Hospice counselors work closely with family and provide follow up grief and other services after the patient dies.

*It's not expensive, it's essentially free.*

Medicare picks up almost all of the charges.

*It's not just pain medication.*

Originally disease fighting medications (as opposed to pain and comfort meds) were *not* given; today, under "open access," the patient can continue some disease-fighting treatment.

*It may not be the end of the road.*

Powerful drugs designed to cure can lead to deathlike symptoms. Once stopped, some patients walk out.

*It's not giving up hope, it's giving up pain, confusion and fear.*

Hospice eliminates pain (they assert that they can be almost 100% effective) and educates the patient and the family about the dying process so that it can be as humane as possible.

People need to think differently about hospice. It is not about giving up on life but giving up on pain, expense and fear. The best thing one can do is to simply ask a hospice nurse to visit the family and patient. Informed decisions, better decisions, can be made.

# Being There and Mourning

*"I'm afraid of dying but terrified of dying alone."*

Be there, even if you don't want to be, even if your thoughts are not loving or profound. It might not be a hallmark moment. To flee sickness and death is instinctive. There may be resentment stemming from prior wrongs; there may be self pity from being left alone; there may be impatience and thoughts of dinner. None of us is as loving, as caring, as we would hope to be. We're human: our fleeting thoughts don't matter; what matters, being bedside.

We crave human contact, physical contact, a caress, a kiss, holding hands. Will they even know you're there? Better than knowing you're not. Hearing goes last: whispering memories, offering encouragement, and, to break the emotional intensity of those moments, telling a great story.

*Voltaire, on his death bed, was urged by a priest "This is the time to denounce Satan." Voltaire refused. "No, this is not the time to be making enemies."*

There will come a time when being there is over; time to return to a life that is the same but somehow different. T.V. tells us that mourning is a process, with marked stages and with final goals. That hasn't been our experience. Mourning is different for all of us. Don't beat yourself up if you aren't doing it right, not feeling the things you think you should.

Mourning is not a process one "works through" to get to some point where it is over, allowing one to "get on with your life." If there is a goal to mourning, it is not to get over the death. It is to *relocate* the loved one—to create a different kind of relationship with the person:

*"So that's what the President said. I wish I could call Dad and get his reaction. What would he say?"*

Depression and great distress are not inevitable. Some grieve before the death and experience the actual death with relief. And there is the background question, "What I am to do now?" Dylan Thomas's wife wrote a book with the haunting title, *Leftover Life to Kill*. Despair mixed with relief; dark, intense moments mixed with daily chores and gossip. Life is always in the *present* tense. There are no rules, no stages, no end points. Best advice: be with friends, neighbors, and relatives. Talk. Cry. Tell jokes.

*An elderly couple sits on the couch. The wife says, "If I die first, you should remarry. If you die first, I'll get a dog."*

*Why are dogs better than husbands? They don't wake you in the middle of the night, "If I die, will you get a new dog?"*

And remember Ashley Montagu's observation: "The idea is to die young as late as possible."

Mourning is not a momentary interruption in life. It continues for the rest of your life. You won't be "OK" for a long time and memories will always rush back, unexpected, more real than the earth you stand on.

In a marvelous poem, *Funeral Blues,* W. H. Auden captures how many feel at the death of a loved one, the initial shock that the world goes on.

*Stop all the clocks, cut off the telephone,*

*Prevent the dog from barking with a juicy bone,*

*Silence the pianos, and with a muffled drum*

*Bring out the coffin, let the mourners come.*

He ends with the feeling of despair:

*The stars are not wanted now; put out every one,*

*Pack up the moon and dismantle the sun;*

*Pour away the ocean and sweep up the wood;*

*For nothing now can ever come to any good.*

Years ago Joe Biden's wife and daughter were killed in a car wreck. No doubt he felt that nothing could ever come to any good. Decades late, as Vice President of the United States, he addressed a gathering of mothers and fathers, sons and daughters, of soldiers who had been killed in Iraq and Afghanistan.

*"I promise you this. There will come a time, I promise you, there will come a time when you think of them, you will smile before you cry."*